WILLIAM HAZLITT

Modern Critical Views

Henry Adams
Edward Albee
A. R. Ammons
Matthew Arnold
John Ashbery
W. H. Auden
Jane Austen
James Baldwin
Charles Baudelaire
Samuel Beckett
Saul Bellow
The Bible
Elizabeth Bishop
William Blake
Jorge Luis Borges
Elizabeth Bowen
Bertolt Brecht
The Brontës
Robert Browning
Anthony Burgess
George Gordon, Lord
   Byron
Thomas Carlyle
Lewis Carroll
Willa Cather
Cervantes
Geoffrey Chaucer
Kate Chopin
Samuel Taylor Coleridge
Joseph Conrad
Contemporary Poets
Hart Crane
Stephen Crane
Dante
Charles Dickens
Emily Dickinson
John Donne & the Seven-
   teenth-Century Meta-
   physical Poets
Elizabethan Dramatists
Theodore Dreiser
John Dryden
George Eliot
T. S. Eliot
Ralph Ellison
Ralph Waldo Emerson
William Faulkner
Henry Fielding
F. Scott Fitzgerald
Gustave Flaubert
E. M. Forster
Sigmund Freud
Robert Frost

Robert Graves
Graham Greene
Thomas Hardy
Nathaniel Hawthorne
William Hazlitt
Seamus Heaney
Ernest Hemingway
Geoffrey Hill
Friedrich Hölderlin
Homer
Gerard Manley Hopkins
William Dean Howells
Zora Neale Hurston
Henry James
Samuel Johnson and
   James Boswell
Ben Jonson
James Joyce
Franz Kafka
John Keats
Rudyard Kipling
D. H. Lawrence
John Le Carré
Ursula K. Le Guin
Doris Lessing
Sinclair Lewis
Robert Lowell
Norman Mailer
Bernard Malamud
Thomas Mann
Christopher Marlowe
Carson McCullers
Herman Melville
James Merrill
Arthur Miller
John Milton
Eugenio Montale
Marianne Moore
Iris Murdoch
Vladimir Nabokov
Joyce Carol Oates
Sean O'Casey
Flannery O'Connor
Eugene O'Neill
George Orwell
Cynthia Ozick
Walter Pater
Walker Percy
Harold Pinter
Plato
Edgar Allan Poe
Poets of Sensibility & the
   Sublime

Alexander Pope
Katherine Ann Porter
Ezra Pound
Pre-Raphaelite Poets
Marcel Proust
Thomas Pynchon
Arthur Rimbaud
Theodore Roethke
Philip Roth
John Ruskin
J. D. Salinger
Gershom Scholem
William Shakespeare
   (3 vols.)
   Histories & Poems
   Comedies
   Tragedies
George Bernard Shaw
Mary Wollstonecraft
   Shelley
Percy Bysshe Shelley
Edmund Spenser
Gertrude Stein
John Steinbeck
Laurence Sterne
Wallace Stevens
Tom Stoppard
Jonathan Swift
Alfred, Lord Tennyson
William Makepeace
   Thackeray
Henry David Thoreau
Leo Tolstoi
Anthony Trollope
Mark Twain
John Updike
Gore Vidal
Virgil
Robert Penn Warren
Evelyn Waugh
Eudora Welty
Nathanael West
Edith Wharton
Walt Whitman
Oscar Wilde
Tennessee Williams
William Carlos Williams
Thomas Wolfe
Virginia Woolf
William Wordsworth
Richard Wright
William Butler Yeats

These and other titles in preparation

Modern Critical Views

WILLIAM HAZLITT

Edited and with an introduction by
Harold Bloom
Sterling Professor of the Humanities
Yale University

CHELSEA HOUSE PUBLISHERS ◇ 1986
New York ◇ New Haven ◇ Philadelphia

© 1986 by Chelsea House Publishers, a division of Chelsea House Educational Communications, Inc.
   133 Christopher Street, New York, NY 10014
   345 Whitney Avenue, New Haven, CT 06511
   5014 West Chester Pike, Edgemont, PA 19028

Introduction © 1986 by Harold Bloom

Printed and bound in the United States of America

∞ The paper used in this publication meets the minimum requirements of the American National Standard for Permanence of Paper for Printed Library Materials, Z39.48-1984.

Library of Congress Cataloging-in-Publication Data
Main entry under title:
William Hazlitt.
      (Modern critical views)
      Bibliography: p.
      Includes index.
      1. Hazlitt, William, 1737–1820—Criticism and interpretation—Addresses, essays, lectures.
I. Bloom, Harold.   II. Series.
PR4773.W44   1986   824'.7   86-920
ISBN 0-87754-685-1 (alk. paper)

863681

Contents

Editor's Note

This book brings together a representative selection of the most distinguished modern literary criticism of the great English Romantic critic, William Hazlitt, arranged in the chronological order of its original publication. I am grateful to Henry Finder for his erudition and insight in helping to locate and choose these essays.

The editor's introduction explains Hazlitt's poetics of power, including his exuberant sense of gusto and his Wordsworthian nostalgia. Stuart M. Tave's analysis of the relation between the psychology of sympathy and the aesthetics of humor in Hazlitt begins the chronological sequence. It is followed here by Christopher Salvesen's moving overview of Hazlitt as "a master of regret," with a particular emphasis upon Hazlitt's triumph as a writer of prose.

Robert Ready's account of Hazlitt's scandalous and pathetic self-revelation, the *Liber Amoris*, returns to the theory of the sympathetic imagination in order to relate the book to the main body of Hazlitt's work. A crucial aspect of that work, Hazlitt's stance as a critic of modern prose fiction and its comic heritage, is interpreted by John Kinnaird as another instance of Hazlitt's central transition from public lecturer to personal essayist, a transition undertaken to preserve Hazlitt's own literary power.

A very different yet as Hazlittian a mode of apprehension is invoked in the British Labor parliamentarian Michael Foot's appreciation, which lauds Hazlitt as the best literary representative of the spirit of the revolutionary age. John L. Mahoney, examining Hazlitt's theory of the imagination, centers upon the critic's de-idealizing sense that the arts were not progressive, rightly seeing in Hazlitt an ancestor of current theories of the darker side of influence and tradition.

This book concludes with two advanced studies of Hazlitt that again find him to be a vital precursor of our current critical concerns. Both are by David Bromwich, a Hazlittian scholar-critic whose work on Hazlitt may prove definitive. Bromwich first analyzes Hazlitt's relation to both Words-worth and Rousseau, showing us how we can read the High Romantic version of the Sublime more generously through Hazlitt's acute sympathy for it, a sympathy more convincing because of Hazlitt's discernments of Romantic limitations. Even more powerfully, Bromwich then meditates upon Hazlitt's intricate sense of the critical balance between quotation and allusion, a balance always at the center of the dialectical link between reading and writing.

Introduction

I

David Bromwich, Hazlitt's best critic, shrewdly says of Hazlitt's key word *gusto* that it "accords nicely with the belief that taste adds to our nature instead of correcting it." I take it that Hazlitt's *gusto* is an aesthetic displacement of the Dissenting Protestant version of grace, which corrects our nature without abolishing it. The son of a radical Dissenting Minister, Hazlitt himself was always a Jacobin with a faith in Napoleon as the true heir of the Revolution. Unswerving in his politics, Hazlitt also remained an unreconstructed early Wordsworthian, unlike Wordsworth himself, a difference that Hazlitt bitterly kept in mind, as here in his observations on Wordsworth's *The Excursion*:

> In the application of these memorable lines, we should, perhaps, differ a little from Mr. Wordsworth; nor can we indulge with him in the fond conclusion afterwards hinted at, that one day *our* triumph, the triumph of humanity and liberty, may be complete. For this purpose, we think several things necessary which are impossible. It is a consummation which cannot happen till the nature of things is changed, till the many become as united as the *one*, till romantic generosity shall be as common as gross selfishness, till reason shall have acquired the obstinate blindness of prejudice, till the love of power and of change shall no longer goad man on to restless action, till passion and will, hope and fear, love and hatred, and the objects proper to excite them, that is, alternate good and evil, shall no longer sway the bosoms and businesses of men. All things move, not in progress, but in a ceaseless round; our strength lies in our weakness; our virtues are built on our vices; our faculties are as limited as our being; nor can we lift man above his nature more than above the earth he

treads. But though we cannot weave over again the airy, unsubstantial dream, which reason and experience have dispelled,

> What though the radiance, which was once so bright,
> Be now for ever taken from our sight,
> Though nothing can bring back the hour
> Of glory in the grass, of splendour in the flower:

yet we will never cease, nor be prevented from returning on the wings of imagination to that bright dream of our youth; that glad dawn of the day-star of liberty; that spring-time of the world, in which the hopes and expectations of the human race seemed opening in the same gay career with our own; when France called her children to partake her equal blessings beneath her laughing skies; when the stranger was met in all her villages with dance and festive songs, in celebration of a new and golden era; and when, to the retired and contemplative student, the prospects of human happiness and glory were seen ascending like the steps of Jacob's ladder, in bright and never-ending succession. The dawn of that day was suddenly overcast; that season of hope is past; it is fled with the other dreams of our youth, which we cannot recall, but has left behind it traces, which are not to be effaced by Birthday and Thanksgiving odes, or the chaunting of *Te Deums* in all the churches of Christendom. To those hopes eternal regrets are due; to those who maliciously and wilfully blasted them, in the fear that they might be accomplished, we feel no less what we owe—hatred and scorn as lasting!

In effect, the aesthetic loss of Wordsworth's visionary gleam is associated here with the spiritual loss of revolutionary hope. All loss, for the critic Hazlitt, is ultimately a loss of gusto, since *gusto* is Hazlitt's version of Blake's "exuberance," as in: "Exuberance is Beauty." One sees this clearly when he transfers the term *gusto* from painters to writers:

The infinite quantity of dramatic invention in Shakespeare takes from his gusto. The power he delights to shew is not intense, but discursive. He never insists on any thing as much as he might, except a quibble. Milton has great gusto. He repeats his blow twice; grapples with and exhausts his subject. His imagination has a double relish of its objects, an inveterate attachment to the things he describes, and to the words describing them.

———Or where Chineses drive
With sails and wind their *cany* waggons *light*.

Wild above rule or art, *enormous* bliss.

There is a gusto in Pope's compliments, in Dryden's satires, and
Prior's tales; and among prose-writers, Boccaccio and Rabelais
had the most of it. We will only mention one other work which
appears to us to be full of gusto, and that is the *Beggar's Opera*.
If it is not, we are altogether mistaken in our notions on this
delicate subject.

Shakespeare's gusto is in his exuberance of invention, Milton's in his
exhaustive tenacity at battering the object, as it were. An aesthetic category
comprehensive enough to include also Pope, Dryden, and Prior, on the one
side, and Boccaccio, Rabelais, and John Gay, on the other, is perhaps too
broad to be of use to practical criticism. Hazlitt's own gusto or critical
exuberance proved capable of overcoming this difficulty, and he gave us a
poetics of power still unsurpassed in its potential:

> The language of poetry naturally falls in with the language of
> power. The imagination is an exaggerating and exclusive faculty:
> it takes from one thing to add to another: it accumulates cir-
> cumstances together to give the greatest possible effect to a fa-
> vourite object. The understanding is a dividing and measuring
> faculty, it judges of things not according to their immediate
> impression on the mind, but according to their relations to one
> another. The one is a monopolising faculty, which seeks the
> greatest quantity of present excitement by inequality and dis-
> proportion; the other is a distributive faculty, which seeks the
> greatest quantity of ultimate good, by justice and proportion.
> The one is an aristocratical, the other a republican faculty. The
> principle of poetry is a very anti-levelling principle. It aims at
> effect, it exists by contrast. It admits of no medium. It is every-
> thing by excess. It rises above the ordinary standard of sufferings
> and crimes. It presents a dazzling appearance. It shows its head
> turretted, crowned, and crested. Its front is gilt and blood-
> stained. Before it "it carries noise, and behind it leaves tears."
> It has its altars and its victims, sacrifices, human sacrifices. Kings,
> priests, nobles, are its train-bearers, tyrants and slaves its exe-
> cutioners.—"Carnage is its daughter."—Poetry is right-royal. It

puts the individual for the species, the one above the infinite-
many, might before right. A lion hunting a flock of sheep or a
herd of wild asses is a more poetical object than they; and we
even take part with the lordly beast, because our vanity or some
other feeling makes us disposed to place ourselves in the situation
of the strongest party. So we feel some concern for the poor
citizens of Rome when they meet together to compare their wants
and grievances, till Coriolanus comes in and with blows and big
words drives this set of "poor rats," this rascal scum, to their
homes and beggary before him. There is nothing heroical in a
multitude of miserable rogues not wishing to be starved, or
complaining that they are like to be so; but when a single man
comes forward to brave their cries and to make them submit to
the last indignities, from mere pride and self-will, our admiration
of his prowess is immediately converted into contempt for their
pusillanimity. The insolence of power is stronger than the plea
of necessity. The tame submission to usurped authority or even
the natural resistance to it has nothing to excite or flatter the
imagination: it is the assumption of a right to insult or oppress
others that carries an imposing air of superiority with it. We had
rather be the oppressor than the oppressed. The love of power in
ourselves and the admiration of it in others are both natural to
man: the one makes him a tyrant, the other a slave.

   This is from Hazlitt's discussion of *Coriolanus* in his *Characters of Shakespear's Plays*. The quality of excess is central to Hazlitt's insight here, which
tells us that meaning gets started (rather than being merely repeated) by
excess, by overflow, and by a sense of potential, a sense of something evermore
about to be. The dialectic of this poetics of power depends upon an interplay
of Shakespearean and Wordsworthian influences upon Hazlitt. From Shakespeare, Hazlitt takes an awareness that character may be fate, yet only
personality bestows some measure of freedom. From Wordsworth, Hazlitt
received a new consciousness of how a writer could begin again despite the
strength and persistence of cultural traditions. The freedom of personality,
in Falstaff, *is* freedom because ego ceases to be persecuted by superego. The
originality of writing, in Wordsworth, is the disappearance of subject matter,
and its replacement by subjectivity. Taken together, the ego of free wit and
the triumph of a fresh subjectivity make up the manner and matter of
Hazlitt's characteristic achievement, an essay at once familiar and critical,
firmly literary yet also discursive and speculative.

In his loving meditation, "On the Periodical Essayists," Hazlitt lists his precursors: Montaigne, Steele (rather than Addison), Johnson (despite Hazlitt's dislike of his style), Goldsmith. Had Edmund Burke been a familiar essayist rather than an orator, Burke certainly would be Hazlitt's nearest ancestor. Instead, Hazlitt makes a second to Johnson in a great procession of critical essayists that goes on to Carlyle, Emerson, Ruskin, Pater, and Wilde. (I omit Coleridge because of his obsession with method, and Arnold because of his authentic incompetence.) The procession ceases in our century because the mode now seems inadequate, not so much to the apparent complexities of modernist literature (after all, many of those now resolve themselves into more complications), but to the waning of the self, with all the perplexities attendant upon that waning. A curious irony of modern literature made Freud, the analyst of such waning, also the only twentieth-century essayist worthy to be the coda of the long tradition that went from Montaigne on through Johnson, Hazlitt, and Emerson until it culminated in Freud's older contemporaries, Ruskin, Nietzsche, and Pater.

II

Hazlitt's poetics of power seems to me more Freudian than any of the psychopoetics—orthodox or Lacanian—that currently drift uselessly in Freud's wake. Like Freud, Hazlitt knows that the poets—Shakespeare, Milton, Wordsworth—were there before him, which is a very different realization than any that penetrate the blindnesses of what now passes for "Freudian literary criticism." The poets are still there before Freud, better guides to the interpretation of Freud than he could ever be to the reading of consciousnesses even more comprehensive and coherent than his own. Hazlitt, in his best theoretical essay, "On Poetry in General," begins with the fine realization: "Poetry then is an imitation of Nature, but the imagination and the passions are a part of man's nature." Passion, or pathos, or sublimity, or power (the four are rightly one, according to Hazlitt) remove poetry from the domain of all conventional considerations of psychology and morality:

> We are as fond of indulging our violent passions as of reading a
> description of those of others. We are as prone to make a torment
> of our fears, as to luxuriate in our hopes of good. If it be asked,
> Why do we do so? the best answer will be, Because we cannot
> help it. The sense of power is as strong a principle in the mind
> as the love of pleasure. Objects of terror and pity exercise the

same despotic control over it as those of love or beauty. It is as natural to hate as to love, to despise as to admire, to express our hatred or contempt, as our love or admiration.

> Masterless passion sways us to the mood
> Of what it likes or loathes.

Not that we like what we loathe; but we like to indulge our hatred and scorn of it; to dwell upon it, to exasperate our idea of it by every refinement of ingenuity and extravagance of illustration; to make it a bugbear to ourselves, to point it out to others in all the splendour of deformity, to embody it to the senses, to stigmatize it by name, to grapple with it in thought, in action, to sharpen our intellect, to arm our will against it, to know the worst we have to contend with, and to contend with it to the utmost. Poetry is only the highest eloquence of passion, the most vivid form of expression that can be given to our conception of anything, whether pleasurable or painful, mean or dignified, delightful or distressing. It is the perfect coincidence of the image and the words with the feeling we have, and of which we cannot get rid in any other way, that gives an instant "satisfaction to the thought." This is equally the origin of wit and fancy, of comedy and tragedy, of the sublime and pathetic. When Pope says of the Lord Mayor's show,—

> Now night descending, the proud scene is o'er,
> But lives in Settle's numbers one day more!

—when Collins makes Danger, "with limbs of giant mould,"

> —Throw him on the steep
> Of some loose hanging rock asleep:

when Lear calls out in extreme anguish,

> Ingratitude, thou marble-hearted fiend,
> How much more hideous shew'st in a child
> Than the sea-monster!

—the passion of contempt in the one case, of terror in the other, and of indignation in the last, is precisely satisfied. We see the thing ourselves, and shew it to others as we feel it to exist, and as, in spite of ourselves, we are compelled to think of it. The imagination, by thus embodying and turning them to shape, gives an obvious relief to the indistinct and importunate cravings of the will.—We do not wish the thing to be so; but we wish it to appear such as it is. For knowledge is conscious power; and the mind is no longer, in this case, the dupe, though it may be the victim of vice or folly.

To speak of poetry as giving "an obvious relief to the indistinct and importunate cravings of the will" is to have more than anticipated Freud. Hazlitt's quotation from *The Merchant of Venice* is the center of one of Shylock's great speeches:

> Some men there are love not a gaping pig;
> Some that are mad if they behold a cat;
> And others, when the bagpipe sings i' th' nose,
> Cannot contain their urine; for affection,
> Mistress of passion, sways it to the mood
> Of what it likes or loathes.

"Masterless passion" is as likely a reading as "Mistress of passion," the text being uncertain, and better suits Hazlitt's emphasis upon the cravings of the will. Hazlittian exuberance, *gusto*, teaches us to admire Shylock even as we admire Coriolanus. Few passages even in Hazlitt are as superbly memorable as when he shows us how the grandest poetry can be the most immoral, here in *Coriolanus*:

> This is but natural, it is but natural for a mother to have more regard for her son than for a whole city; but then the city should be left to take some care of itself. The care of the state cannot, we here see, be safely entrusted to maternal affection, or to the domestic charities of high life. The great have private feelings of their own, to which the interests of humanity and justice must courtesy. Their interests are so far from being the same as those of the community, that they are in direct and necessary opposition to them; their power is at the expense of *our* weakness; their riches of *our* poverty; their pride of *our* degradation; their splendour of *our* wretchedness; their tyranny of *our* servitude. If they had the superior knowledge ascribed to them (which they have not) it would only render them so much more formidable; and from Gods would convert them into Devils. The whole dramatic moral of *Coriolanus* is that those who have little shall have less, and that those who have much shall take all that others have left. The people are poor; therefore they ought to be starved. They

are slaves; therefore they ought to be beaten. They work hard;
therefore they ought not to be treated like beasts of burden. They
are ignorant; therefore they ought not to be allowed to feel that
they want food, or clothing, or rest, that they are enslaved,
oppressed, and miserable. This is the logic of the imagination
and the passions; which seek to aggrandize what excites admiration, and to heap contempt on misery, to raise power into
tyranny, and to make tyranny absolute; to thrust down that which
is low still lower, and to make wretches desperate; to exult mag-
istrates into kings, kings into gods; to degrade subjects to the
rank of slaves, and slaves to the condition of brutes. The history
of mankind is a romance, a mask, a tragedy, constructed upon
the principles of *poetical justice*; it is a noble or royal hunt, in
which what is sport to the few is death to the many, and in
which the spectators halloo and encourage the strong to set upon
the weak, and cry havoc in the chase though they do not share
in the spoil. We may depend upon it that what men delight to
read in books, they will put in practice in reality.

Though Hazlitt is an intellectual of the permanent Left, of the French
Revolution, he is too great a critic not to see that poetry worships power
without regard to the morality of power. Indeed, his poetics of power compels
us to see more than that, which is that Plato was right in fearing Homer's
effect upon society. Poetical justice is antithetical to societal justice, and
the noble or royal hunt of the imagination does not make us better citizens
or better human beings, and very likely may make us worse.

III

Hazlitt, like Johnson before him, and the great progression of Carlyle,
Emerson, Ruskin, Pater, and Wilde after him, teaches us several unfash-
ionable truths as to the nature of authentically *literary* criticism. It must be
experiential; it must be at least somewhat empirical or pragmatic; it must
be informed by love for its subject; above all it must follow no method
except the personality of the critic himself. Coleridge never ceased to quest
for method, and lost the critical gift in consequence, while Matthew Arnold
drowned what gift he had by assuring himself that they handled these matters
better on the Continent. Hazlitt is a literary critic; our contemporary imitators of Continental philosophy may be human scientists or ideological
rebels or what they will, but they are not literary critics. Hume's philosophy

teaches the critic to fall back upon personality because every other possibility has been collapsed by skepticism. German thought persuaded Coleridge to posit an "organic" unity in imaginative works, but such organicism and its resultant unities can be seen now as banal fictions. Hazlitt, like Johnson, refuses to carry philosophical aesthetics into the pragmatic realms of criticism. I read Coleridge when and as I have to, but I read Hazlitt for pleasure and insight. Whether he writes on "The Indian Jugglers" or "On Going a Journey" or "On a Sun-Dial," Hazlitt reminds us always that life and literature are, for him, the one interpenetrated reality.

I remember "The Indian Jugglers" partly for its vivid celebration of the jugglers' skill:

> Coming forward and seating himself on the ground in his white dress and tightened turban, the chief of the Indian Jugglers begins with tossing up two brass balls, which is what any of us could do, and concludes with keeping up four at the same time, which is what none of us could do to save our lives, nor if we were to take our whole lives to do it in. Is it then a trifling power we see at work, or is it not something next to miraculous? It is the utmost stretch of human ingenuity, which nothing but the bending the faculties of body and mind to it from the tenderest infancy with incessant, ever-anxious application up to manhood, can accomplish or make even a slight approach to. Man, thou art a wonderful animal, and thy ways past finding out! Thou canst do strange things, but thou turnest them to little account!—To conceive of this effort of extraordinary dexterity distracts the imagination and makes admiration breathless. Yet it costs nothing to the performer, any more than if it were a mere mechanical deception with which he had nothing to do but to watch and laugh at the astonishment of the spectators. A single error of a hair's-breadth, of the smallest conceivable portion of time, would be fatal: the precision of the movements must be like a mathematical truth, their rapidity is like lightning. To catch four balls in succession in less than a second of time, and deliver them back so as to return with seeming consciousness to the hand again, to make them revolve round him at certain intervals, like the planets in their spheres, to make them chase one another like sparkles of fire, or shoot up like flowers or meteors, to throw them behind his back and twine them round his neck like ribbons or like serpents, to do what appears an impossibility, and to do it with

all the ease, the grace, the carelessness imaginable, to laugh at, to play with the glittering mockeries, to follow them with his eye as if he could fascinate them with its lambent fire, or as if he had only to see that they kept time with the music on the stage—there is something in all this which he who does not admire may be quite sure he never really admired anything in the whole course of his life. It is skill surmounting difficulty, and beauty triumphing over skill.

Remarkable as descriptive writing, this acquires hidden power when subsequently it is revealed as a literary paradigm, leading Hazlitt to the profound observation: "No act terminating in itself constitutes greatness." The act of writing *Paradise Lost* is precisely one that does not terminate in itself. Hazlitt's insight is that the canon is constituted by works that engender further works that do not terminate in themselves. "On Going a Journey" begins by advising that "the soul of a journey is liberty, perfect liberty, to think, feel, do just as one pleases." A few pages later the essay achieves perceptions into our involuntary perspectivism that both anticipate and correct Nietzsche:

There is hardly anything that shows the short-sightedness or capriciousness of the imagination more than travelling does. With change of place we change our ideas; nay, our opinions and feelings. We can by an effort indeed transport ourselves to old and long-forgotten scenes, and then the picture of the mind revives again, but we forget those that we have just left. It seems that we can think but of one place at a time. The canvas of the fancy has only a certain extent, and if we paint one set of objects upon it, they immediately efface every other. We cannot enlarge our conceptions; we only shift our point of view. The landscape bares its bosom to the enraptured eye; we take our fill of it; and seem as if we could form no other image of beauty or grandeur. We pass on, and think no more of it; the horizon that shuts it from our sight also blots it from our memory like a dream. In travelling through a wild barren country, I can form no idea of a woody and cultivated one. It appears to me that all the world must be barren, like what I see of it. In the country we forget the town, and in town we despise the country. "Beyond Hyde Park," says Sir Fopling Flutter, "all is a desert." All that part of the map that we do not see before us is a blank. The world in our conceit of it is not much bigger than a nutshell. It is not one prospect expanded into one another, county joined to county, kingdom to kingdom, lands to seas, making an image voluminous and vast; the mind can form no larger idea of space than the eye can take in at a single glance. The rest is a name written on a map, a calculation of arithmetic. For instance, what is the true signification of that immense mass of territory and population, known by the name of China to us? An inch of paste-board on a wooden globe, of no more account than a China orange! Things near us are seen of the size of life: things at a distance are diminished to the size of the understanding. We measure the universe by ourselves, and even comprehend the texture of our own being only piece-meal.

"On a Sun-Dial" is a nostalgic reverie explaining why Hazlitt has never bothered to own a watch or a clock. In the midst of this brief study of the nostalgias, we are suddenly given a memorable theory of romance, as applicable to Hawthorne as to Wordsworth:

Surely, if there is anything with which we should not mix up our vanity and self-consequence, it is with Time, the most independent of all things. All the sublimity, all the superstition that hang upon this palpable mode of announcing its flight, are chiefly attracted to this circumstance. Time would lose its abstracted character, if we kept it like a curiosity or a jack-in-a-box: its prophetic warnings would have no effect, if it obviously spoke only at our prompting, like a paltry ventriloquism. The clock that tells the coming, dreaded hour—the castle bell, that "with its brazen throat and iron tongue, sounds one unto the drowsy ear of night"—the curfew, "swinging slow with sullen roar" o'er wizard stream or fountain, are like a voice from other worlds, big with unknown events. The last sound, which is still kept up as an old custom in many parts of England, is a great favourite with me. I used to hear it when a boy. It tells a tale of other times. The days that are past, the generations that are gone, the tangled forest glades and hamlets brown of my native country, the woodsman's art, the Norman warrior armed for the battle or in his festive hall, the conqueror's iron rule and peasant's lamp extinguished, all start up at the clamorous peal, and fill my mind with fear and wonder. I confess, nothing at present interests me but what has been—the recollection of the impressions of my early life, or events long past, of which only the dim traces remain in a smouldering ruin or half-obsolete custom. That *things should be that are now no more*, creates in my mind the most unfeigned astonishment. I cannot solve the mystery of the past, nor exhaust my pleasure in it.

One sees, after reading this, why Wordsworth's "Ode: Intimations of Immortality" was Hazlitt's poem-of-poems, as it was Emerson's and Ruskin's. Hazlitt's regret is hardly for actual immortality, which he dismisses with splendid vigor in his "On the Fear of Death." It is rather what he adumbrates in his superb "On the Feeling of Immortality in Youth":

Objects, on our first acquaintance with them, have that singleness and integrity of impression that it seems as if nothing could destroy or obliterate them, so firmly are they stamped and rivetted on the brain. We repose on them with a sort of voluptuous indolence, in full faith and boundless confidence. We are absorbed in the present moment, or return to the same point—idling away a great deal of time in youth, thinking we have enough and to spare. There is often a local feeling in the air, which is as fixed as if it were of marble; we loiter in dim cloisters, losing ourselves in thought and in their glimmering arches; a winding road before us seems as long as the journey of life, and as full of events. Time and experience dissipate this illusion; and by reducing them to detail, circumscribe the limits of our expectations. It is only as the pageant of life passes by and the masques turn their backs upon us, that we see through the deception, or believe that the train will have an end. In many cases, the slow progress and monotonous texture of our lives, before we mingle with the world and are embroiled in its affairs, has a tendency to aid the same feeling. We have a difficulty, when left to ourselves, and without the resource of books or some more lively pursuit, to "beguile the slow and creeping hours of time," and argue that if it moves on always at this tedious snail's-pace, it can never come to an end. We are willing to skip over certain portions of it that separate us from favourite objects, that irritate ourselves at the unnecessary delay. The young are prodigal of life from a superabundance of it; the old are tenacious on the same score, because they have little left, and cannot enjoy even what remains of it.

As a commentary upon our common experience, both when young and when old, this compels the chill of a self-recognition beyond illusion and

delusion alike. But it is also a powerfully implicit commentary upon Wordsworth's Great Ode, and upon very nearly everything else in Wordsworth
that truly matters. Hazlitt's strength, matched among critics in the language
only by Johnson and by Ruskin, is that he never allows us to forget the
dark and antithetical relationship between the power of the imagination and
the power of human experience. Imaginative gain and experiential loss are
identical in Hazlitt, who, unlike Wordsworth, understands that there is no
knowledge that is not purchased by the loss of power, no power that is not
purchased at the expense both of others and of the self.

STUART M. TAVE

Antipathetic and Sympathetic

The mingling of levity and gravity—of tragedy and comedy, of spleen and humor, of laughter and tears, and the closely allied use of the comic as defense or escape—found further expression in the development of the eighteenth-century theory of "sympathy." It was partly through the agency of that theory that humor and pathos made their alliance, though, as was generally true of the relations of philanthropy and comedy, sympathy was also a strongly anticomic force.

In a simple form, sympathy is the natural reflex whereby one man shares the emotions of another. Hutcheson, attempting to claim laughter for the benevolists, we recall, had pointed out that "like other Affections, it is very contagious; our whole Frame is so sociable, that one merry Countenance may diffuse Chearfulness to many." Hartley, having accounted for the origin of laughter in children by his theory of the "nascent cry," then added, however, that their progress in learning is much accelerated by imitation: they learn to laugh as they learn to walk and talk, and laugh most when they see other laugh. "The same thing is evident even in Adults; and shews us one of the Sources of the sympathetic Affections." Or as Abraham Tucker said in his chapter on sympathy (1768), "it has been observed a thousand times that laughter and yawning generally go round the company." It is unlikely that Tucker had read a sixteenth-century Frenchman, Laurent Joubert, who had said the same thing (and then added in a marginal note, "& quelquefois on pisse par cōpagnie") because, as he said, it was a common observation.

From *The Amiable Humorist*. © 1960 by the University of Chicago. The University of Chicago Press, 1960.

But it was under the leadership of the Scottish philosophers of the eighteenth century, Hume, and especially Adam Smith and his successors, that sympathy became an essential force in both ethical action and aesthetic creation. It operates by the imagination. It enables us to place ourselves, by sympathetic imagination, in the position of others and thus to feel intimately their passions and sensations: this identification is basic in ethical action; it also enables a great poet like Shakespeare to create imagined characters, by convincing representation from within and not by a merely external description of emotion. In the early nineteenth century Hazlitt was the major expositor of the sympathetic imagination: it is passion, the fundamental cause of human action, that sets the imagination to work, and it is through the imagination that we can project ourselves sympathetically into the passions of others. The more intense our sympathy, the more complete our comprehension of the man or object before us will be, and the more closely we approach moral perfection, and aesthetic genius. For in the arts it is "an intense sympathy with some one beauty or distinguishing characteristic in nature" that constitutes "rare genius." Shakespeare, who was unique, had a "perfect sympathy with all things." "He had only to think of any thing in order to become that thing, with all the circumstances belonging to it."

But the concept of sympathy is of only limited use in the explanation of laughter. Tears are easily accounted for; distress evokes distress; or as Hume said, " 'TWILL be easy to explain the passion of *pity*, from the precedent reasoning concerning *sympathy*." There are occasions, however, when one sees a fellow creature in distress and laughs outright, the very reverse of the usual fellow feeling. This laughter is entirely different from every other human emotion with any pretense to the amiable and is plainly the result of a failure of sympathy. The simplest reaction of anyone who places a high value on sympathy is to reject laughter, as Shaftesbury did. Adam Smith (1759) also suggests the malevolent nature of laughter. A small vexation in another excites no sympathy, he says, because our sympathetic passions are not as strong as our original passions. "There is, besides, a malice in mankind, which not only prevents all sympathy with little uneasinesses, but renders them in some measure diverting. Hence the delight which we all take in raillery." It was Smith, in a later edition of *The Theory of Moral Sentiments*, who began the legend that Gray might have become the first poet of the English language if his sensibility had not been so much hurt by a foolish and impertinent parody that he virtually stopped writing.

This titbit was snapped up by Richard Payne Knight, and in his *Analytical Inquiry into the Principles of Taste* (1805) Knight wrote a thorough-going case against laughter as the antithesis of sympathy: "laughter is an expression of joy and exultation; which arises not from sympathy but triumph; and which seems therefore to have its principle in malignity." As opposed to tragedy, which heightens and embellishes human nature, comedy exposes and exaggerates its weaknesses and defects, exhibits peculiarities and perversions, and degrades us. The mock-heroic, which Knight associates with humor, amuses by novelty and contrast "and flatters that innate principle of selfish vanity or malignity, which makes us naturally delight in the degradation of whatsoever is exalted." Parody is the easiest of tricks, as the ridiculous is always lying in wait on the verge of the sublime and pathetic: "a single low word or incongruous circumstance is sufficient to sink into meanness and ridicule the most lofty imagery, or pathetic effusion."

There were not very many who wrote in this heavy style; generally it was accepted that, for good or bad, the various forms of the comic depended upon the rupture of sympathy. Thus Abraham Tucker said that we laugh at follies and blunders because they imply a deliberate effort to attain a purpose by ineffective means: the earnestness and expectation in the persons so laboring for their purpose fill "our own imagination by sympathy with the like ideas, which are immediately dissipated upon the reflection of their being ineffectual and nugatory." And just as disproportion, the reduction of grandeur and dignity, distinguishes the witty from the sublime, as George Campbell had said, the reduction of sympathy distinguishes the humorous from the pathetic. "A just exhibition of any ardent or durable passion, excited by some adequate cause," according to Campbell, "instantly attacheth sympathy, the common tie of human souls, and thereby communicates the passion to the breast of the hearer." But when the passion is slight or transient, or its motive is imaginary, or when it displays itself preposterously, "a natural representation, instead of fellow-feeling, creates amusement, and universally awakens contempt. The portrait in the former case we call *pathetic*, in the latter *humorous*." Hazlitt certainly knew Tucker's work—one of his first publications was an abridgment of it—and he had read Campbell too. On the first page of the *Lectures on the Comic Writers* (1819) we read: "We shed tears from sympathy with real and necessary distress; as we burst into laughter from want of sympathy with that which is unreasonable and unnecessary." Follies, absurdities, and odd accidents afford us amusement from the rejection of "false claims upon our sympathy, and end in laughter."

If everything that went wrong, Hazlitt continues, every vanity or weakness in another, gave us a sensible pang, life would be hard. But as long as the immediate oddity of a situation, or as long as the absurdity of a foolish action, is the most striking thing in it, "the ludicrous prevails over the pathetic, and we receive pleasure instead of pain from the farce of life which is played before us." Thus laughter is at times a protective barrier for the sympathetic as for the splenetic man; they were close relatives. Beattie, in his chapter "Of Sympathy" (*An Essay on Poetry and Music*, 1776), had justified Shakespeare's mixture of tragedy and comedy because this great man's powers in the pathetic were such that had he made his tragedies uniform "no person of sensibility would have been able to support the representation."

> I can never accuse of indecency the man, who, by the introduction of a little unexpected merriment, saves me from a disordered head, or a broken heart. If Shakespeare knew his own powers, he must have seen the necessity of tempering his tragic rage, by a mixture of comic ridicule; otherwise there was some danger of his running into greater excesses than deer-stealing, by sporting with the lives of all the people of taste in these realms.

But the value of the comic in this scheme of things is clearly its subordinate utility. It is auxiliary to higher and better emotions, and, with Beattie, functions rather like a spiritual smelling bottle. Shakespeare tempers his tragic rage lest he overpower the person of sensibility, he says, on the same principle that the farcical afterpiece of a tragedy revives the spirits. One doesn't choose to go home with the gloom of an affecting tragedy upon his mind, and if the play has been soundly instructive there is no risk that its value will be dissipated by "a little innocent mirth." A little innocent mirth can hardly dissipate, because it is so feeble and so easily stifled when it threatens to step beyond its little area, "the inward emotion that prompts to laughter is not very powerful; many other emotions have naturally more strength, and have therefore a natural right to suppress it." Consequently, incongruities that rouse pity, moral disapprobation, and the like are not laughable because the weaker emotion gives place to the greater and more important.

The interest of the words is not their novelty—for at least since Aristotle it had been pointed out continually that if a deformity causes pain, it is not ludicrous—but their emphasis. The emphasis is on the "natural right" of the other emotions to suppress laughter, because of the nature of man, or at least what the nature of man ought to be. The "ludicrous sentiment," as Beattie calls it, is not only weak but it "never should be strong"; moral disapprobation "in every mind ought to be, and in every sound mind is, the most powerful principle of the human constitution." Butler and Smollett have perhaps reached the limits of comedy when they find something ludicrous in a wooden leg, for normally we expect, because "we know it is natural," that "pity should prevail over the ludicrous emotion."

With a man of an uncompromising sensibility and sympathy, like Archibald Alison (1790), the argument comes full circle to a latter-day case against tragicomedy. Tragedy is "the highest and noblest species" of drama and it is painful to us, "in the midst of our admiration or our sympathy, and while our hearts are swelling with tender or with elevated emotions," to be forced to descend to the consideration of the mean and indifferent or the ludicrous.

> It is hence that Tragi-comedy is utterly indefensible, after all that has been said in its defence. . . . there is no man of the most common sensibility, who does not feel his mind revolt and his indignation kindle at the absurdity of the Poet, who can thus break in upon the sacred retirement of his sorrow, with the intolerable noise of vulgar mirth.

Hazlitt's concept of tragedy and mirth and of their relationship is not so narrow and unfruitful as this. For him there is more than vulgar mirth in *Lear*: "the sense of sympathy" roused by the contrast of Lear's passions and his daughters' stony hearts "would be too painful, the shock too great, but for the intervention of the Fool, whose well-timed levity comes in to break the continuity of feeling when it can no longer be borne"; the "imagination is glad to take refuge" in the "half-comic, half-serious comments . . . just as the mind under the extreme anguish of a surgical operation vents itself in sallies of wit." And there is more than the mild dissipation of a little innocent mirth, because while the Fool diverts the too great intensity of our disgust with the daughters' treatment of their father, he is also indispensable in that he "carries the pathos to the highest pitch of which it is capable, by shewing the pitiable weakness of the old king's conduct and its irretrievable consequences in the most familiar point of view." Hazlitt's passions are not so squeamish as Alison's or Beattie's. More than that, the strength of his appetite for comedy in general can hardly be appreciated without reading the criticism of his immediate predecessors or contemporaries on some of the writers who delighted him, or contemporary criticism of his enthusiasms. But to him, too, tragedy was a higher art than comedy, and though this in itself was certainly a feeling not limited to him or his age, the manner in which he derives the necessarily lower nature of the comic is characteristic of his age and it is descendent from the late eighteenth-century account of the importance of the sympathetic imagination in poetics and in ethics. Hazlitt's ideas are worth pursuing in some detail, because they reveal a few of the reasons for what has been called "romantic seriousness" and also indicate the kind of comedy that "romantic" criticism could best illuminate.

For Hazlitt the prime motive forces in human life are the passions and the imagination. Perception and action are inevitably and properly given form and significance by them. In that sense poetry is the stuff of life and all men are continually shaping things according to their passions and imagination. Poetry, as an art, is the most perfect language by which these forces express themselves; it emerges when the intensity of passion takes possession of the mind and molds all elements—sensations, feelings, thoughts, and sounds—into a single, harmonious, sustained, and continuous whole. There is room here for "rich, exuberant satire," to which Hazlitt responded warmly, or fine, snarling invective, in which he was expert. But as a reading of *Lear* brings home so forcibly, "the greatest strength of genius is shewn in describing the strongest passions"; the highest form of poetry is "the most impassioned species of it," tragedy, which strives to carry us to "the utmost point of sublimity or pathos." The great moral effect of tragedy is that "it substitutes imaginary sympathy for mere selfishness. It gives us a high and permanent interest, beyond ourselves, in humanity as such."

The comic deliberately reverses all these primary values of continuity and intensity and sympathy. The serious is the habitual stress the mind lays upon the expectation of a regular order of events in which it has an interest: the pathetic or tragic increases this stress "beyond its usual pitch of intensity"; the ludicrous, or comic, loosens or relaxes it "below its usual pitch of intensity." The essence of the laughable is "the incongruous, the disconnecting of one idea from another, or the jostling of one feeling against another," "the solution of continuity in the chain of our ideas . . . [the] *discontinuous*." Laughter is the rejection of sympathy, the prevalence of the ludicrous over the pathetic—and properly so when the claim upon sympathy is false or absurd—but we laugh also at deformity and at mischief, to show our self-satisfaction and contempt for others, to conceal envy or ignorance.

> We laugh at that in others which is a serious matter to ourselves;
> because our self-love is stronger than our sympathy. . . . Some
> one is generally sure to be the sufferer by a joke. What is sport
> to one, is death to another.

Wit and humor, comparatively speaking, "appeal . . . to our indolence, our vanity, our weakness, and insensibility; serious and impassioned poetry appeals to our strength, our magnanimity, our virtue, and humanity."

One notable feature of the *Lectures on the English Comic Writers* is a persistent tendency to run off the subject, to turn from the comic to the contrasting superior realm of "poetry" or "passion" or "imagination." Thus the lecture on Hogarth concludes, inevitably it seems, with a lengthy exposition of "another, mightier world," the "ideal" and "poetical," the world of Raphael. The longest quotation from Congreve is twenty-six lines of *The Mourning Bride*, to show how bad it is: deprived of his wit, "His serious and tragic poetry is frigid and jejune to an unaccountable degree." As for the character of Millamant, it is the finest of its kind and no more can be done with it, but its kind is inferior because "The springs of nature, passion, or imagination are but feebly touched"; it is not so with Rosalind or Perdita. Butler's treatment of the sunrise, in a burlesque simile that had been a stock illustration of incongruity in eighteenth-century analyses of laughter, is here followed by a pair of more pleasant, powerful, and imaginative Spenserian stanzas on the same subject. Lucian gets only a few lines, passing mention of his wit, and high praise because "his comic productions are interspersed with beautiful and eloquent descriptions, full of sentiment, such as"—and here, unhappily, he cites a fable now considered to be certainly spurious. The proper praise of Boccaccio is not that he is a teller of idle jests but "the most refined and sentimental of all the novel-writers."

The lecture on Shakespeare is introduced by a quick knock-down of Dr. Johnson, who thought that Shakespeare's comedies were better than his tragedies because Shakespeare was more at home in comedy: to Hazlitt this merely displays Johnson's "general indisposition to sympathise heartily and spontaneously with works of high-wrought passion or imagination." Shakespeare is the only tragic poet of the world, who treads the utmost bound of nature and passion and lays open all the faculties of the human soul "to act, to think, and suffer, in direst extremities"; but in comedy, wonderful and delightful as he is, he has his superiors, his equals, and many close competitors. "He put his strength into his tragedies, and played with comedy. He was greatest in what was greatest; and his *forte* was not trifling." He was primarily a poet: "his imagination was the leading and master-quality of his mind, which was always ready to soar into its native element: the ludicrous was only secondary and subordinate." His comedies, then, begin to be great when they cease to be comic: "with what freshness and delight we come to the serious and romantic parts! What a relief they are to the mind, after those of mere ribaldry and mirth!"

The manner in which the comic deliberately reverses the higher poetic mode is most evident in wit. Wit is the application of the wrong end of the magnifier to the world of nature and passion: as distinguished from poetry, it is "the imagination or fancy inverted," so applied as to diminish further the little or the mean, or to reduce our emotional response to the lofty and impressive, "instead of producing a more intense admiration and exalted passion, as poetry does." Pope is a great wit; he lacks Shakespeare's "intuitive and mighty sympathy" with the heart of man: the power of his mind is the power of indifference, his excellence lies chiefly in diminishing objects, checking enthusiasm, "sneering at the extravagances of fancy and passion, instead of giving a loose to them." Butler, another great wit, compares the Bear turning round the polestar to a bear tied to a stake: "There cannot be a more witty, and at the same time degrading comparison." The poetry of Milton is greater than *Hudibras* because Milton "aggrandises our notions of human nature" and Butler "degrades" human nature. Butler's characters are mere "nicknames, and bugbears of popular prejudice and vulgar cant, unredeemed by any virtue, or difference or variety of disposition." A nickname is a monstrous thing—Hazlitt was obsessed by the subject and "nickname" is not a term he uses lightly—because it reduces an individual to an abstraction of insignificance.

> Individuals are concrete existences, not arbitrary denominations
> or nicknames; and have innumerable other qualities, good, bad,
> and indifferent, besides the damning feature with which we fill
> up the portrait or caricature, in our previous fancies.

Knowledge of real character in its thousand complexities, anomalies, and redeeming points must be particular, and sympathy is the inevitable consequence. Hazlitt repeats, as he does on at least seven other occasions, " 'the web of our lives is of a mingled yarn, good and ill together' ": this was "truly and finely said long ago, by one who knew the strong and weak points of human nature," but those who classify by nicknames have never learned its meaning. Not to appreciate the existence of the web of mingled yarn is to be deficient in imagination, in sympathetic understanding; and it is in such soil that ridicule flourishes best. Women as a class, for example, have little imagination; they are pure egoists and cannot go out of themselves. One result is that "Women have a quicker sense of the ridiculous than men, because they judge from immediate impressions, and do not wait for the explanation that may be given of them."

Excellence in the comic, clearly, when the comic is anti-sympathetic and anti-imaginative, is something less than genius of a high order. William Duff had devoted a section of his *Essay on Original Genius* (1767) to the distinction between genius on the one hand and wit and humor on the other. Significantly enough, to make his point Duff separates "fancy" from "imagination," in what has been called the first distinct crystallization of these terms. Wit and humor are produced by a "RAMBLING and SPORTIVE Fancy," often superficial, genius "proceeds from the copious effusions of a plastic Imagination." It follows that not every great wit will be a great genius nor every genius a wit. Swift was not a genius, "at least of a very EXALTED kind," Ossian was not a wit. Leigh Hunt in an early book of theatrical criticism (1807) demonstrated that among actors "a great tragedian is a finer genius than a great comedian," because the comedian can observe the habits of daily life but the tragedian requires more imagination to conceive the extraordinary passions of the characters he portrays. Similarly, Hunt informs us, Hogarth is inferior to Michaelangelo, Butler to Milton, Congreve to Shakespeare; Swift is probably the greatest wit that ever lived, but he will never have the reputation of Milton or Shakespeare. Even among schoolboys, those of a "serious and romantic" disposition, who prefer Homer and Sophocles to Terence and Plautus, promise greater genius than those who excel in humor and mimicry. Humor never elevates as imagination does, and the tragic actor, as he has more imagination, has a "more *poetical* genius" than the comedian. Imaginative poetry, Hazlitt says, is superior to ludicrous wit because

> it is easier to let down than to raise up, to weaken than to strengthen, to disconnect our sympathy from passion and power, than to attach and rivet it to any object of grandeur or interest, to startle and shock our preconceptions by incongruous and equivocal combinations, than to confirm, enforce, and expand them by powerful and lasting associations of ideas, or striking and true analogies.

Excellence within the realm of the comic—the scale by which one establishes its subdivisions and their virtues—is determined by this conception of its general nature. The most complete type of comedy is the most completely unsympathetic. The first degree of the laughable, Hazlitt says, "the most shallow and short-lived," is found in a simple surprise, a merely accidental contradiction between our expectations and the events. Above this, "more deep and lasting," is "the ludicrous," which involves character or situation, and where the contradiction is heightened and more impressive because it is an unaccountable deviation from what is customary or desirable. The "highest degree" is "the ridiculous," which is contrary to sense and reason; where the ludicrous arises from improbability, the ridiculous arises from absurdity as well, a defect of a man's own seeking. It is the "most refined of all," and "properly the province of satire," but it is not always so pleasant as the ludicrous "because the same contempt and disapprobation which sharpens and subtilises our sense of the impropriety, adds a severity to it inconsistent with perfect ease and enjoyment."

The ludicrous and the ridiculous, further, are co-ordinate with two

periods of social history, each with its characteristic form of comedy. In the
first "the foibles and follies of individuals are of nature's planting, not the
growth of art or study"; these individuals are unconscious of their defects,
or do not care who knows them, and since they make no attempt at con-
cealment or imposition, when they are represented on the stage

> the spectators rather receive pleasure from humouring the incli-
> nations of the persons they laugh at, than wish to give them pain
> by exposing their absurdity. This may be called the comedy of
> nature, and it is the comedy which we generally find in
> Shakespear.

This is followed by a society in which people become self-conscious and
affected, attempt to disguise their peculiarities and absurdities, pretend to
be what they are not. The object of comedy in this society is to detect these
disguises and to "make reprisals" by exposing them "as severely as possible,"
denying the characters any merit. "This is the comedy of artificial life, of
wit and satire, such as we see it in Congreve, Wycherley, Vanbrugh, etc."
The very success of this comedy in exposing and driving out obvious affectation helps to introduce a third period in which all materials of comic
character, natural and artificial, have been neutralized and there is "no
comedy at all—but *the sentimental*," the modern. The "best" comedy is that
of the second age, "the golden period," because it is the comedy of ridicule.
The fools in Wycherley and Congreve are of their own or of one another's
making, entitled to no quarter and receiving none. "They think themselves
objects of envy and admiration, and on that account are doubly objects of
our contempt and ridicule." It is only the vanity and affectation of the
artificial society that can produce truly contemptible animals, and it is not
until that age is reached that we find "the most pungent ridicule" and "the
keenest edge of satire."

Shakespeare's comedy is not the best because it is too sympathetic and
too poetic. It is sweet and pleasant. "It aims at the ludicrous rather than
the ridiculous. It makes us laugh at the follies of mankind, not despise
them, and still less bear any ill-will towards them." The characters themselves could not be offended at the amusement he draws from their foibles
because "he rather contrives opportunities for them to shew themselves off
in the happiest lights, than renders them contemptible in the perverse
construction of the wit or malice of others." Even in the very best of his
comedies "the spirit of humanity and the fancy of the poet greatly prevail
over the mere wit and satire. . . . we sympathise with his characters oftener
than we laugh at them. His ridicule wants the sting of ill-nature." He aims,

instead, at innocent mirth. In a word, Hazlitt does not consider comedy "as exactly an affair of the heart or the imagination," and it is for this reason that he thinks Shakespeare's comedies deficient.

But it is for this reason only, he is explicit. It has been said that Hazlitt may have been blind to the excellences of Shakespearean comedy, but it is plain that in practice he finds it far more attractive than that comedy which is in theory the best but which is actually less enjoyable. The epithets cannot be mistaken: the fault of Shakespeare's comic muse is that it is "too good-natured and magnanimous. . . . it does not take the highest pleasure in making human nature look as mean, as ridiculous, and contemptible as possible, [as does the comedy of] a later, and (what is called) a more refined period." Shakespeare's comedy of nature is "pastoral and poetical."

> Folly is indigenous to the soil, and shoots out with native, happy, unchecked luxuriance. . . . Nothing is stunted by the churlish, icy hand of indifference or severity. . . . In a word, the best turn is given to every thing, instead of the worst. There is a constant infusion of the romantic and enthusiastic, in proportion as the characters are natural and sincere: whereas, in the more artificial style of comedy, every thing gives way to ridicule and indifference, there being nothing left but affectation on one side, and incredulity on the other.

Restoration comedy, as we have seen, is attractive to him not so much for the reasons of its theoretical superiority as for its romance-like qualities. He likes Farquhar because his heroes are romantic, not knavish, because we have more sympathy with them than with Vanbrugh's heroes, and because of what are evidently Farquhar's good-natured and good-humored Shakespearean traits in making us laugh from pleasure oftener than from malice. And, in fact, he says he is not willing to give a preference to any comedies over Shakespeare's. His preferences have outrun his theory of the comic.

The theory will account for the ridiculous and the satirical, not for the ludicrous and the good-natured; it accounts for artifice and fancy, not for nature and imagination; for contempt, not sympathy; for wit, not humor. But in fact humor embodied all the higher poetic values.

As Dennis, Corbyn Morris, and others had said, wit is impersonal, but humor partakes of the character of the speaker, is individual and particular. This was a commonplace. It was still being repeated, at the end of the eighteenth and the beginning of the nineteenth century, by a critic as obscure as Arthur Browne or a critic like Coleridge. Because it takes its quality from personal, human traits, where wit is fragmentary, detached, cold, fanciful, humor may well be affectionate and sympathetic, mindful of human complexity and dignity. Thomas Tyers (1783), praising Addison, in comparison with Swift, says that wit was more predominant in Swift, humor in Addison; one of the many parallels that follow is that Addison meant to dignify man and Swift to degrade. Duff, too, though he relates "wit and humour" to fancy, throughout most of his demonstration of their inferiority to imagination and genius speaks in fact only of "wit"; moreover, he draws this distinction between wit and humor: wit discovers itself in smart repartees, in ingenious conceits, in fanciful allusions, but humor deals with follies, foibles, and oddities of character, and "Sometimes the character may be so amiable, that its little peculiarities, instead of lessening our esteem or affection, increase the former, and conciliate the latter." The peculiarities must be "innocent in themselves, and indicate or imply genuine excellence"; one instance is the character of Sir Roger de Coverley, "drawn with the most exquisite humour, and by the happiest effort of ADDISON's delicate pencil." Lord Woodhouselee (Alexander Tytler), who seems to have read Duff, takes occasion in his life of Kames (1807) to register his disagreement with both Kames and Campbell on the subject of humor. Humor in the humorist, they both had said, is ridiculous and awakens contempt. Contempt, Woodhouselee replies, is always accompanied by a degree of dislike or aversion; "but a humorous character may, on the contrary," even while he amuses us, "strongly conciliate our affection, our esteem, and even our respect." Sir Roger, Isaac Bickerstaff of the *Tatler* and Uncle Toby are examples, as are also, he feels, Smollett's Tom Bowling and Morgan. "In these characters, humour is associated with a degree of dignity, which is absolutely exclusive of the emotion of contempt." Occasionally, he admits, humor and meanness, hence contempt, may be combined; and he lumps Falstaff with Bardolph and Bobadil as examples. But in such cases the contempt

> seems to lessen, and derogate from, the purer pleasure we receive
> from the equally ludicrous characters in which it has no place.
> To be highly pleased with the expression of any emotion, we
> must completely sympathise with the person who displays it: but
> the feeling of contempt is in a great degree hostile to sympathy.

Humor, partaking of humanity, deriving, as Coleridge said, in its original sense, from a pathology, is a "growth from within." It is natural, unembellished, unrepressed. In Hazlitt's distinction, humor describes "the ludicrous as it is in itself"; wit exposes it by comparison or contrast with something else. "Humour is, as it were, the growth of nature and accident; wit is the product of art and fancy." Furthermore, as the growth of nature and accident, humor is picturesque. This is important in rendering it sympathetic. The "keenness" of all emotions, as Beattie had said, "is in proportion to the vivacity of the perceptions that excite them." We cannot sympathize with what we have never experienced, and conversely, the more we know of an object the more likely we are to sympathize. Consequently the poet strives to be as "vivid and picturesque" as possible, to present the object to the reader in its full form. To Hazlitt, who applies this principle to the comic, an author like Butler fails because the manners of his time seem rather to have irritated him than to have "drawn forth his powers of picturesque imitation." The failure is apparent if we compare him to Cervantes. *Hudibras* is perhaps "the greatest single production of wit" in England, but there is little humor or feeling. "Humour is the making others act or talk absurdly and unconsciously: wit is the pointing out and ridiculing that absurdity consciously, and with more or less ill-nature." Humor requires picturesque imitation, requires sympathy. "Indeed, it requires a considerable degree of sympathy to enter into and describe to the life even the ludicrous eccentricities of others, and there is no appearance of sympathy or liking to his subject in Butler." Thus humor, unlike wit, is feeling, and appeals to feeling. When Keats dined with a company of wits, Horace Smith and others, they only served to convince him "how superior humour is to wit in respect to enjoyment—These men say things which make one start, without making one feel."

And finally, it follows that humor, involving the total being, both of the object and the creator, is deeper, more comprehensive, imaginative. An essayist of *Blackwood's*, in 1820, draws out the conclusion quite well:

> The truth is, that humour is a far higher power than wit, and frequently draws its material from far deeper sources in human nature. The *humours* of mankind are not only endless, but in their most interesting exhibitions they are inseparably blended with their affections, their happiness, and their whole moral as well as natural being. . . . Men of real wit have been more numerous in the world than men of real humour—just as men of fancy have been more numerous than men of imagination.

Carlyle identified humor with genius, wit with talent, and Coleridge, too, noted the connection of humor and genius. It is a relationship we will have to return to. Humor could meet every test.

CHRISTOPHER SALVESEN

A Master of Regret

*A treatise on the Millennium is dull; but who was ever weary of reading
the fables of the Golden Age?*
—"On the Past and Future"

Hazlitt was a master of regret who by force of intellect and style became
the best prose writer of his age. He was the second son of a Dissenting
Minister active in "the cause of civil and religious liberty." In 1783, when
Hazlitt was five, his father embarked for America, whose independence he
had supported; official hostility to his protests for the better treatment of
nearby American prisoners hastened his departure. Hazlitt's father failed to
establish himself as a Unitarian preacher, and four years later the family
returned to England, to the village of Wem in Shropshire. Independence,
the idea of freedom, Hazlitt knew from childhood, and the Fall of the Bastille
in 1789 confirmed this knowledge.

> For my part, I set out in life with the French Revolution, and
> that event had considerable influence on my early feelings, as on
> those of others. Youth was then doubly such. It was the dawn
> of a new era, a new impulse had been given to men's minds, and
> the sun of Liberty rose upon the sun of Life in the same day, and
> both were proud to run their race together. Little did I dream,
> while my first hopes and wishes went hand in hand with those
> of the human race, that long before my eyes should close, that

From *Selected Writings of William Hazlitt*. © 1972 by Christopher Salvesen. Signet/New
American Library, 1972. Originally entitled "Introduction."

dawn would be overcast, and set once more in the night of despotism—"total eclipse!"

["On the Feeling of Immortality in Youth"]

Hazlitt's response to his age was simple. He would never accept the disillusionment and the political reaction which followed the Revolution and the ambitions of Napoleon. He clung to his first ideals. He remained a radical, a Jacobin. Napoleon was his hero; Waterloo was a disaster. The restoration of the Bourbons and the Divine Right of Kings was an abomination. Hazlitt as a child had glimpsed the Millennium; as he advanced in life, it receded and took on the coloring of a Golden Age. But he revived the memory of it continuously, actively, in his writing.

Hazlitt's life is easily enough recorded. The year after the Bastille fell, provincial life at Wem was enlivened by a stay in Liverpool, where he heard sermons and went to the theater. He was a pious and intelligent child. At fourteen, the strains of adolescence and independent thinking made themselves felt. He went to the Unitarian College at Hackney near London, produced an outline of "A New Theory of Civil and Criminal Legislation" (which his tutor "good-naturedly accepted in lieu of the customary *themes*"), and resolved not to become a Dissenting Minister. He came home and spent two years reading: the English poets and novelists, Burke, Junius, Rousseau. Then occurred one of the most important events in Hazlitt's life. "Never, the longest day I have to live, shall I have such another walk as this cold, raw, comfortless one, in the winter of the year 1798." This January walk took Hazlitt to hear Coleridge preach. What this led to "My First Acquaintance with Poets" makes clear: "that my understanding . . . did not remain dumb and brutish, or at length found a language to express itself, I owe to Coleridge." Throughout Hazlitt's writing he addresses Coleridge with a deep sense of intellectual and emotional debt—often mixed with a sense of betrayal in Coleridge's apostasy from Revolution to Reaction. He visited Coleridge in the spring, met Wordsworth and Dorothy, and "had free access" to the *Lyrical Ballads*, "which were still in manuscript."

Though a reader and a thinker, Hazlitt was by no means yet a writer. Following his elder brother, John, he decided to be a painter—unenthusiastically. Then about a year after Hazlitt met Coleridge came another revelation. He saw in London an exhibition of old Italian masters—Titians, Raphaels. "I was staggered when I saw the works there collected, and looked at them with wondering and with longing eyes. A mist passed away from my sight. . . . A new sense came upon me." He applied himself intensely, he copied Rembrandts, he painted portraits. In 1802 he went to Paris, to the Louvre hung with the Italian spoils of Napoleon: another revelation to which he often recurs. "Here, for four months together, I strolled and studied, and daily heard the warning sound—*'Quatre heures passées, il faut fermer, Citoyens'* (Ah! why did they ever change their style?) muttered in coarse provincial French." Gradually Hazlitt convinced himself he would never become a great painter; but his portrait of Charles Lamb (1804, in the National Portrait Gallery, London) is proof that he was a good one. Painfully, Hazlitt had written his first book, *An Essay on the Principles of Human Action* (1805); dry but firm about man's essential disinterested goodness, he opposes the mechanistic philosophies of his time.

For the next few years, Hazlitt's literary life is miscellaneous: a political pamphlet, an abridgement, a selection, a reply to Malthus, an English grammar, the editing and completion of a memoir. He is friendly with Charles and Mary Lamb; they introduce him to Sarah Stoddart; he marries her in 1808. She was three years older than Hazlitt, with short hair, with a small private income and a cottage in the village of Winterslow on the edge of Salisbury Plain which provided him with a working retreat.

In 1812 Hazlitt delivered his course of lectures on English Philosophy and began his career in journalism. He started as a parliamentary reporter for *The Morning Chronicle*, the leading Whig paper, the opposite of *The Times*. But he soon branched out; he contributed some short essays in the eighteenth-century style, a caustic note on Southey, and some dramatic criticism. He added political and art criticism and other pieces. Mary Russell Mitford records of the editor "the doleful visage with which Mr. Perry used to contemplate the long column of criticism, and how he used to execrate 'the d——d fellow's d——d stuff' for filling up so much of the paper in the very height of the advertisement season." Perry then seems to have behaved rather badly and "turned him off." This directed Hazlitt to the columns of *The Examiner*, the lively and important radical weekly edited by John and Leigh Hunt. (They had already served their two-year prison sentences for remarking of the Prince Regent, amongst other things, that "This Adonis in loveliness was a corpulent man of fifty.") *The Examiner*, Bentham noted in 1812, "is the one that at present, especially among the high political men, is most in vogue. It sells already between 7,000 and 8,000." In 1814, in *The Examiner*, appeared Hazlitt's first masterpiece of criticism, his account of Wordsworth's *Excursion*. His growing reputation was confirmed when toward the end of the year he was invited to contribute to the *Edinburgh Review*.

For about the next four years Hazlitt's activity as a literary journalist is at its height. He is art and drama critic of a new paper, *The Champion*;

he produces *The Round Table* ("A Collection of Essays on Literature, Men, and Manners") and the *Characters of Shakespear's Plays*; he is a tireless political commentator and aligns himself even more resolutely on the Radical side, in his association with John Hunt and *The Examiner*. In 1818 he incurred the unwelcome attentions of the Tory *Quarterly Review* and of *Blackwood's*. The crudest demarcations of politics lie behind the meaningless abuse which these journals (especially the latter in the persons of John Wilson and J. G. Lockhart) launched at "the Cockney School"—Keats, Hazlitt, and (more understandably) Leigh Hunt. There was barely an inkling of literary criticism, but much irresponsible malice and invective. Hazlitt was able to take care of himself, as in his *Letter to William Gifford* ("Sir—You have an ugly trick of saying what is not true of anyone you do not like; and it will be the object of this letter to cure you of it."). As for *Blackwood's*, Hazlitt threatened a lawsuit which was settled out of court in his favor. But despite his resilience, he found the attacks deeply wounding in their blatant untruthfulness; while a hostile *Quarterly* review of the *Characters of Shakespear's Plays* put a complete stop—so his publishers told him—to its previously successful sale.

In January 1818 Hazlitt had embarked on his three series of lectures on English literature. The popularity of lectures was fairly recent; the lecture was a kind of democratic education especially for those who wanted to pursue "the career open to talent." Hazlitt contributes much to this new form. He had obviously thought about it: he varies the pace, knowing that no audience can concentrate solidly; his lectures, though full of thinking, do not have the close dialectic of the essays. He offers copious quotation, reading out in full, for example, "Tam o' Shanter" ("I shall give the beginning of it, but I am afraid I shall hardly know when to leave off") or "Hart-Leap Well" ("As Mr Wordsworth's poems have been little known to the public, or chiefly through garbled extracts from them, I will here give an entire poem."). Hazlitt describes his basic approach to lecturing:

> what I have undertaken to do . . . is merely to read over a set
> of authors with the audience, as I would do with a friend, to
> point out a favourite passage, to explain an objection; or if a
> remark or a theory occurs, to state it in illustration of the subject,
> but neither to tire him nor puzzle myself with pedantic rules and
> pragmatical *formulas* of criticism that can do no good to anybody
> . . . In a word, I have endeavoured to feel what was good, and
> to "give a reason for the faith that was in me."
>
> *Lectures on the Age of Elizabeth*

But they are not as informal as all that; they are deliberate, they have plenty of intellectual attack. Crabb Robinson complained of one set of lectures by Coleridge (who was a pioneer in the field) that each was an "immethodical rhapsody"—a danger Hazlitt avoided, partly by reading his lectures. Of his first one on philosophy, Robinson complained that Hazlitt had "no conception of the difference between a lecture and a book." But Hazlitt took advice, improved his manner, and in his later series engaged the active participation of his audience. The staid Crabb Robinson himself was provoked: "He was so contemptuous, speaking of [Wordsworth's] letter about Burns, that I lost my temper and hissed." Thomas Noon Talfourd has left the most interesting account of the lectures. Hazlitt, he remarks, had but "an imperfect sympathy" with his hearers: "They consisted chiefly of Dissenters, who agreed with him in his hatred of Lord Castlereagh, but who "loved no plays"; of Quakers, who approved him as the opponent of Slavery and Capital Punishment, but who "heard no music"; of citizens devoted to the main chance, who had a hankering after the "improvement of the mind," but to whom his favourite doctrine of its natural disinterestedness was a riddle; of a few enemies, who came to sneer; and a few friends, who were eager to learn and to admire." Among these latter was Keats, whose greatest poetry echoes again and again, faintly but unmistakably; with signs of how attentively he listened. Talfourd continues:

> The comparative insensibility of the bulk of his audience to his finest passages, sometimes provoked him to awaken their attention by points which broke the train of his discourse, after which he could make himself amends by some abrupt paradox which might set their prejudices on edge, and make them fancy they were shocked. He startled many of them at the onset, by observing that, since Jacob's dream, "the heavens have gone further off, and become astronomical"—a fine extravagance, which the ladies and gentlemen who had grown astronomical themselves under the preceding lecturer, felt called on to resent as an attack on their severer studies. When he had read a well-known extract from Cowper, comparing a poor cottager with Voltaire, and had pronounced the line, "A truth the brilliant Frenchman never knew," they broke into a joyous shout of self-gratulation, that they were so much wiser than a wicked Frenchman. When he passed by Mrs. Hannah More with observing that "she had written a great deal which he had never read," a voice gave expression to the general commiseration and surprise, by calling out "More

pity for you!" They were confounded at his reading with more emphasis, perhaps, than discretion, Gay's epigrammatic lines on Sir Richard Blackmore, in which scriptural persons are freely hitched into rhyme; but he went doggedly on to the end, and, by his perseverance, baffled those who, if he had acknowledged himself wrong by stopping, would have hissed him without mercy.

Talfourd concludes: "He was not eloquent in the true sense of the term; for his thoughts were too weighty to be moved along by the shallow stream of feeling which an evening's excitement can arouse. He wrote all his lectures, and read them as they were written; but his deep voice and earnest manner suited his matter well."

With the publication of his collected *Political Essays* in 1819 Hazlitt signaled his retirement from political journalism. His engagement by John Scott of the *London Magazine* in 1820, first to write monthly surveys of the drama, and then to contribute "Table Talks," marks the beginning of Hazlitt's final great decade. In August of this year Hazlitt began his involvement with Sarah Walker, the daughter of a tailor in whose house he lodged (he now lived apart from his wife). Sarah Walker was a dull girl—scrawny, intellectually inert—about whom Hazlitt worked himself into a romantic frenzy. She gave him neither rebuffs nor real encouragement. His infatuation has something willed in it, as well as intense suffering. He went to Edinburgh to make use of the easier Scottish divorce laws, but once fully separated from his wife, he found that Sarah Walker was unobtainable at any price. All that was left was to record the whole affair in the *Liber Amoris*. But nothing could stop him writing: he had written over fifty "Table Talks" in two years; the rest of his life was almost equally industrious, and comparatively uneventful. He married again in 1824, a widow who stayed with him three years. He toured France and Italy with her; he lived for some time in Paris collecting material for his *Life of Napoleon*. This gigantic compilation is fairly described as an apologia for his own life, if we remember that Hazlitt's Napoleon-worship was politically rather than psychologically inspired. In 1822 he had written:

> There are some persons of that reach of soul that they would like to live two hundred and fifty years hence, to see to what height of empire America will have grown up in that period, or whether the English constitution will last so long. These are points beyond me. But I confess I should like to live to see the downfall of the Bourbons. That is a vital question with me; and I shall like it the better, the sooner it happens!

He just lived to see it, to have his faith in freedom confirmed. As he put it in "Personal Politics," one of his last essays, "The Revolution of the Three Days was like a resurrection from the dead, and showed plainly that liberty too has a spirit of life in it." Hazlitt's last words, recorded by his son, were "Well, I've had a happy life." His writings confirm this: despite the years of inarticulateness, of hackwork, despite his precarious career, the malicious attacks and the quarrels, despite the disappointment of his ideals and longings.

The vitality, the mixture of application and spontaneity in all his writing, was not always immediately apparent in the man himself. But from Coleridge's impression of him in 1803—"brow-hanging, shoe-contemplative, *strange*"—our views of Hazlitt's demeanor and temperament are consistent enough, making allowance for whether friend or foe is talking, and for some increase in his self-confidence and reputation. Benjamin Haydon has an amusing account of his visit to the christening of Hazlitt's son in 1813. No dinner when he arrived:

> At last came in a maid who laid a cloth and put down knives and forks in a heap. Then followed a dish of potatoes, cold, waxy and yellow. Then came a great bit of beef with a bone like a battering-ram, toppling on all its corners. Neither Hazlitt nor Lamb seemed at all disturbed, but set to work helping each other; while the boy, half-clean and obstinate, kept squalling to put his fingers into the gravy.—Even Lamb's wit and Hazlitt's disquisitions, in a large room, wainscotted and ancient, where Milton had meditated, could not reconcile me to such violation of all the decencies of life.

In this room of august literary memories, Hazlitt scribbled notes above the mantelpiece. Bryan Waller Procter recorded his first meeting:

> At the time I refer to (it must, I think, have been in the year 1816) he was publishing, in the *Examiner*, some of his papers called "The Round Table." His name was not so extensively circulated then as it since has been; but he was, nevertheless, well known to be a first-rate critic in matters connected with art and the theatres; and by his associates (some of them not too ready to admit the claims of literary candidates) he was characterized as an acute and profound thinker. His countenance did not belie this opinion. His figure was indeed indifferent, and his movements shy and awkward; but there was something in his earnest irritable face, his restless eyes, his black hair, combed

backwards and curling (not too resolutely) about a well-shaped
head, that was very striking.

Procter comments elsewhere: "At home, his style of dress (or undress) was
perhaps slovenly, because there was no one to please; but he always presented
a very clean and neat appearance when he went abroad. His mode of walking
was loose, weak and unsteady; although his arms displayed strength, which
he used to put forth when he played at racquets with Martin Burney and
others. He played in the old Fives Court (now pulled down) in St. Martin's
Street; and occasionally exhibited impatience when the game went against
him." Diffident but irascible, a man of concealed nervous energy, committed
to ideas and abstractions, caring little for bourgeois comforts, Hazlitt clung
to his personality: "We had as lief *not be as not be ourselves*" ("On the Fear of
Death," 1822). His happiness lay in the accumulated identity of his hard
life.

After Wordsworth, Hazlitt draws more fully on the sense of the past
than any other English Romantic. All the same, the prime quality of Hazlitt's
imagination is an energetic delight in ideas and their working-out. Ideas
have a life of their own; Hazlitt's great virtue is to make them personal
without reducing their vitality. A nostalgic temperament combines with
supremely incisive thinking. This is not a matter of contrast; Hazlitt works
with ideas which he has made his own through years of rehearsal. He knows
and loves the repetitions of the mind, "still occupied with something interesting, still recalling some old impression, still recurring to some difficult
question and making progress in it, every step accompanied with a sense of
power." ("On the Past and Future"). He *owns* his speculations no less than
his particular memories. For example, at the end of "A Farewell to Essay-
Writing" (1828) he recalls a time when he used to walk out in the evenings
with Charles and Mary Lamb,

> to look at the Claude Lorraine skies over our heads, melting from
> azure into purple and gold, and to gather mushrooms, that sprung
> up at our feet, to throw into our hashed mutton at supper . . .
> It is in looking back to such scenes that I draw my best consolation
> for the future. Later impressions come and go, and serve to fill
> up the intervals; but these are my standing resource, my true
> classics.

And he continues, still sounding the note of regret inseparable from such
memories: "If I have had few real pleasures or advantages, my ideas, from
their sinewy texture, have been to me in the nature of realities; and if I

should not be able to add to my stock, I can live by husbanding the interest." His ideas have become almost a physical part of him ("I have brooded over an idea till it has become a kind of substance in my brain").

For Hazlitt, ideas are emotions; often reflected on, they remain ideas, opinions deeply grounded, forcefully put; yet they also come across with the impact of feelings. This may remind us of what T. S. Eliot discovered in early seventeenth-century poetry, "a direct sensuous apprehension of thought or a recreation of thought into feeling." But in the essays not only are ideas emotions, but we feel how these ideas have *become* emotions, in the strictly Romantic mode of growing. And yet their immediate coming across in Hazlitt's prose is what counts; there is no "dissociation of sensibility." The gap is closed, thanks to another feeling Hazlitt imparts, that of ideas *still* developing, "every step accompanied with a sense of power"; more generally, it is due to his remarkable ability to make thought and feeling cohere in the total form of an essay. One of the pleasures of a Hazlitt essay is to feel the "sinewy texture" of ideas both intellectually and emotionally, to be aware of ideas in action and of Hazlitt "husbanding the interest" on them.

The sequence of a Hazlitt essay, like the syntax of the Metaphysicals, displays "fidelity to thought and feeling." It is an epitome of past and present; it works because Hazlitt is confidently grounded in what he calls "continuity of impression." After years of hard thinking and writing, Hazlitt need not always distinguish sharply between feelings and ideas. According to Eliot, "there are traces of a struggle toward unification of sensibility" in one or two passages of Shelley and Keats. But Wordsworth came nearest to solving the essentially new problem: how to combine thinking and feeling with the added Romantic dimension—and difficulty—of memory. Hazlitt applies this mode to himself and to more purely intellectual material. Wordsworth's poetry combines the "sensuous and intellectual" being—subjectively. Hazlitt solves that closely connected Romantic problem, the proper relation of Sense and Sensibility.

Whether fusing them or, as he sometimes does, distinguishing carefully between them, he gets the proportions right. The backward look, so often an invitation to sensibility and nothing more, provides the main impulse of Hazlitt's continued intellectual activity. He refers throughout the essays of the last decade to his feeling for time. "As we advance in life, we acquire a keener sense of the value of time. Nothing else, indeed, seems of any consequence; and we become misers in this respect" ("On the Feeling of Immortality in Youth," 1827). He celebrates the more philosophical applications too: "Time, like distance, spreads a haze and a glory round all things. Not to perceive this, is to want a sense, is to be without imagination"

("On Antiquity," 1821). Hazlitt makes full use of this sense, indulging it, controlling it.

Regret, for Hazlitt, is a matter of temperament, something inherent. It crops up, for example, in his early *Reply to Malthus* (1807) in a characteristic confessional interlude: "I never fell in love but once . . . it was like a vision, a dream, like thoughts of childhood, an everlasting hope, a distant joy, a heaven, a world that might be. The dream is still left, and sometimes comes confusedly over me in solitude and silence, and mingles with the softness of the sky, and veils my eyes from mortal grossness." But it appears more in connection with the French Revolution and the disappointment of the hopes then aroused. Other private occasions may have compelled Hazlitt's backward look but it is first fully invoked by the large public events of his time. It appears strongly, for example, in a letter of 1814 to the *Morning Chronicle* where Hazlitt offers a definition of a "true Jacobin" as someone who "has seen the evening star set over a poor man's cottage, or has connected the feeling of hope with the heart of man, and who, though he may have lost the feeling, has never ceased to reverence it" (he uses the image again in "On the Pleasure of Painting"). It appears at greater length in his review of *The Excursion*, where he laments "that spring-time of the world, in which the hopes and expectations of the human race seemed opening in the same gay career with our own . . ." It may have fled; but it "has left behind traces. . . . To those hopes eternal regrets are due." Pastoral regret seems inseparable from any imaginative response to contemporary politics—think of George Eliot or even of George Orwell. This kind of personal-political regret is Hazlitt's own version of the Romantic sense of onwardness and fading: like Wordsworth, he is left with "the memory of what has been and never more will be."

From 1820 onward Hazlitt the essayist claims the right to reverie. The tone may be relaxed, but the claim is serious. "I conceive that the past is as real and substantial a part of our being, that it is as much a *bona fide*, undeniable consideration in the estimate of human life, as the future can possibly be." The past may be gone:

> but it *has had* a real existence, and we can still call up a vivid recollection of it as having once been . . . Let us not rashly quit our hold upon the past, when perhaps there may be little else left to bind us to existence. Is it nothing to have been, and to have been happy or miserable? . . . Or, to use the language of a fine poet (who is himself among my earliest and not least painful recollections)—

> What though the radiance which was once so bright
> Be now for ever vanish'd from my sight,
> Though nothing can bring back the hour
> Of glory in the grass, of splendour in the flow'r—

yet am I mocked with a lie, when I venture to think of it?

These lines from the "Immortality Ode" are one of Hazlitt's talismanic quotations; the examples of Wordsworth or of Rousseau are frequently in his mind when he looks back. "It is the past that gives me most delight and most assurance of reality"; he continues,

> What to me constitutes the great charm of the Confessions of Rousseau is their turning so much upon this feeling. He seems to gather up the past moments of his being like drops of honeydew to distil a precious liquor from them . . . was he not to live the first and best part of it over again, and once more be all that he then was?

His enthusiasm is partly based on literary-cum-temperamental affinities. How far does he actually resemble him? He is, Irving Babbitt notes, one of Rousseau's "chief disciples in the art of impassioned recollection." Rousseau obviously helped to form Hazlitt's own use of his past; and, unlike Wordsworth, he was one of Hazlitt's most pleasurable recollections. Of *The New Eloise* and the *Confessions* Hazlitt recalled: "We spent two whole years in reading these two works; and," he adds, "in shedding tears over them . . . They were the happiest years of our life. We may well say of them, sweet is the dew of their memory and pleasant the balm of their recollection!" He prefers the *Confessions* "because it contains the fewest set paradoxes or general opinions. It relates entirely to himself; and no one was ever so much at home on this subject as he was. From the strong hold which they had taken of his mind, he makes us enter into his feelings as if they had been our own, and we seem to remember every incident and circumstance of his life as if it had happened to ourselves." In his *Round Table* essay on Rousseau Hazlitt writes,

> The only quality which he possessed in an eminent degree, which alone raised him above ordinary men, and which gave to his writings and opinions an influence greater, perhaps, than has been exerted by any individual in modern times, was extreme sensibility, or an acute and even morbid feeling of all that related to his own impressions, to the objects and events of his own life.

> He had the most intense consciousness of his own existence. No
> object that had once made an impression on him was ever after
> effaced. Every feeling in his mind became a passion. His craving
> after excitement was an appetite and a disease. His interest in
> his own thoughts and feelings was always wound up to the highest
> pitch; and hence the enthusiasm which he excited in others.

Like Rousseau, Hazlitt had an "intense consciousness of his own existence."
But he is much less of an exhibitionist: his one foray in this direction, the
Liber Amoris, is an aberration, though interesting both psychologically and
artistically as a "documentary." He is also against the Wordsworthian "egotistical sublime." He may impart an air of self-indulgence to his more
personal moments; his tone is quite different from Wordsworth's philosophical meditations on his own being. He does not use himself in the
solemn "representative" manner of Wordsworth; nor does he justify himself
in Rousseau's spirit of informative "confessional" self-revelation. At an appropriate point in an essay, Hazlitt turns to his past in a short controlled
episode of intensified feeling. He is in many ways remarkably reticent. He
has little to say about his childhood; he records only one memory of his
years in America. "The taste of barberries which have hung out in the snow
during the severity of a North American winter, I have in my mouth still,
after an interval of thirty years; for I have met with no other taste, in all
that time, at all like it." Hazlitt presents it mainly as a psychological
curiosity. It is the complete opposite of Proust tasting his madeleine: for
Hazlitt nothing has been forgotten, nothing revived. "It remains by itself,
almost like the impression of a sixth sense." But in the same essay ("Why
Distant Objects Please") Hazlitt evokes a different kind of memory, dating
from immediately after his return from America, which is rich, evocative,
and especially Proustian in being so deeply incorporated as to be involuntary.
"When I was quite a boy, my father used to take me to the Montpelier Tea-
gardens at Walworth. Do I go there now? No; the place is deserted, and
its borders and its beds o'erturned." But it lives in his memory.

> A new sense comes upon me, as in a dream; a richer perfume,
> brighter colours start out; my eyes dazzle; my heart heaves with
> its new load of bliss, and I am a child again. My sensations are
> all glossy, spruce, voluptuous, and fine: they wear a candied coat,
> and are in holiday trim. I see the beds of larkspur with purple
> eyes; tall holy-oaks, red and yellow; the broad sunflowers, caked
> in gold, with bees buzzing round them; wildernesses of pinks,
> and hot-glowing pionies; poppies run to seed; the sugared lily,

and faint mignionette, all ranged in order, as thick as they can grow; the box-tree borders; the gravel-walks, the painted alcove, the confectionary, the clotted cream—I think I see them now with sparkling looks; or have they vanished while I have been writing this description of them? No matter; they will return again when I least think of them.

The poetic Hazlitt takes his part with the psychologist who remembered the taste of barberries. But where Wordsworth remembered himself as a naked five-year-old, or went back more mystically to infancy and birth, Hazlitt's sense of origin is fixed in adolescence and youth, in the period of intellectual excitement and growth.

The Romantic problem was how best to make use of an "intense consciousness of existence"—what sort of form to put it in. Rousseau's *Confessions*, Wordsworth's *Prelude*, Byron's *Childe Harold* are some of the answers; the Hazlitt essay is another. The expression of personality is the purpose and controlling factor of the essay. Egotism, therefore, cannot be avoided; but the personality is integrated with the chosen form. Montaigne, says Hazlitt, "whom I have proposed to consider as the father of this kind of personal authorship among the moderns . . . was a most magnanimous and undisguised egotist." Hazlitt values Montaigne's egotism. He recommends him "to anyone to read who has ever thought at all, or who would learn to think justly on any subject"; and he himself must have learnt much about the individual *tone* of thought. He celebrates him as "the first who had the courage to say as an author, what he felt as a man." His great virtue lay in "merely daring to tell us whatever passed through his mind, in its naked simplicity and force, that he thought any ways worth communicating." Montaigne claims: "I describe not the essence, but the passage . . . from day to day, from minute to minute." Montaigne presents himself as an unpremeditated creature, a mind at work. Hazlitt likewise shows us a mind in action, but one which is backward-looking too, drawing on "standing resources" and "true classics"—that is the Romantic difference. Yet you could also claim for Hazlitt in his essays what Dr. Johnson claimed for Burke's conversation: "His stream of mind is perpetual." There is nothing random, no mere "stream of consciousness"—but the sense of momentum is important.

Hazlitt combines the force of mind and interest in self of Montaigne with something of the observant sensibility of Addison and Steele. That is partly why, both as social and literary critic, he understands the eighteenth century, why he is so good on Fielding, Hogarth, Crabbe. He responds fully to the demands of realism, to the world created by the novelists; at the same time, he maintains his absolute attachment to "the ideal," that world "which exists only in conception and in power, the universe of thought and senti-ment, that surrounds and is raised above the ordinary world of reality." He is not an urbane writer; he is however urban, a Londoner, and as he observes,

> In London there is a *public*; and each man is part of it . . . We have a sort of abstract existence; and a community of ideas and knowledge (rather than local proximity) is the bond of society and good-fellowship. This is one great cause of the tone of political feeling in large and populous cities. There is here a visible body-politic, a type and image of that huge Leviathan the State. We comprehend that vast denomination, the *People*, of which we see a tenth part daily moving before us.

This kind of insight gives a special quality to Hazlitt's role (which he assigns to the essayist in general) of "moral historian." Hazlitt, commentator and censor, observes the political behavior of his contemporaries with a new sort of intellectual penetration. He introduces in one essay a story of Wordsworth and some inconsistent behavior concerning candles by saying that he will "give some instances of a change in sentiment in individuals, which may serve for materials of a history of opinion in the beginning of the 19th century":

> (A gentleman went to live, some years ago, in a remote part of the country, and as he did not wish to affect singularity he used to have two candles on his table of an evening. A romantic acquaintance of his in the neighbourhood, smit with the love of simplicity and equality, used to come in, and without ceremony snuff one of them out, saying, it was a shame to indulge in such extravagance, while many a poor cottager had not even a rush-light to see to do their evening's work by. This might be about the year 1802, and was passed over as among the ordinary oc-currences of the day. In 1816 (oh! fearful lapse of time, pregnant with strange mutability), the same enthusiastic lover of economy, and hater of luxury, asked his thoughtless friend to dine with him in company with a certain lord, and to lend him his man servant to wait at table; and just before they were sitting down to dinner, he heard him say to the servant in a sonorous whisper— 'and be sure you don't forget to have six candles on the table!'
> ["On Consistency of Opinion"])

It is an original concept, "a history of opinion"; in *The Spirit of the Age* Hazlitt himself goes some way toward writing it. "The spirit of the age" is likewise a new concept (you can't imagine Dr. Johnson considering it a useful subject for discussion). What is signficant about Hazlitt's rendering of something so cloudy and Teutonic is that he does it in terms of individuals; the dangers of "totalitarian" thinking are avoided. He refuses to offer any systematic definition; he is interested in the variety of human example. Yet his ability to attempt the "extensive view" is important. His comprehensive mixture of principle and his own personality gives his work a literary tone which does not exist in any previous age. Neither *philosophe* nor journalist, Hazlitt combines a little of each in his continual task of self-expression and the creation of lasting work.

The Hazlitt essay is one of the great formal achievements of English Romanticism. The form derives from Hazlitt's presence therein; he creates an authentic mode of shaping experience. "I have turned for consolation to the past, gathering up fragments of my early recollections, and putting them into a form that might live." We need not overemphasize the word "form" here; but Hazlitt pursues form unequivocally. It is sometimes remarked that he is at his best in small-scale works; but small is a relative term, and the Hazlitt essay (running to 7,000–8,000 words) is, by any standards applicable to the form in general, immense. At the same time it should be granted that the true scale of the essay is intimate; it is a personal colloquial mode. The essay is particularly interesting in being essentially discursive while at the same time being one of the most musical of prose forms. Its changes of mood and style (see, for example, "On the Feeling of Immortality in Youth") trace a rhythmic pattern which can be felt whole by the reader. Hazlitt once called his essays "these voluntaries of composition": one way of thinking of them formally, though used with some self-disparagement. He talked in similar terms of Coleridge's Watchman and Friend pieces; "whoever will be at pains to examine them closely, will find them to be *voluntaries*, fugues, solemn capriccios, not set compositions with any *malice prepense* in them, or much practical meaning." (Hazlitt's criticism of Coleridge often has this "symbolist" touch. Of "Kubla Khan" he writes: "It is not a poem, but a musical composition"; and he characterizes Coleridge as "the man of all others . . . to write marginal notes without a text"—which sounds like an adumbration of his alignment in Symbolist tradition, or the matter of a poem by Wallace Stevens.) The formal pattern of a Hazlitt essay is really a question of what Hazlitt had heard Coleridge propound, "the metaphysical distinction between the grace of form, and the grace that arises from motion."

Style—the manner in which Hazlitt gets on with his argument and brings forward his personality—further defines the structure. Hazlitt the stylist is characterized by the title of his last collection of essays—the Plain Speaker. He is a rhetorician, concerned with the different ways of using language and of combining them effectively. He is interested in the musical qualities of prose, in rhapsody and exclamatory flights. But what he aims at most often is plain-speaking—the frank expression of opinion in straightforward language. This, Hazlitt knows, is difficult. His ideal is a "pure conversational prose-style"; hard to achieve because the exact word must always be found—the approximations of actual talk will not do:

> There is a research in the choice of a plain, as well as of an ornamental or learned style; and, in fact, a great deal more. Among common English words, there may be ten expressing the same thing with different degrees of force and propriety, and only one that answers exactly with the idea we have in our minds. Each word in familiar use has a different set of associations and shades of meaning attached to it . . . it is in having the whole of these at our command, and in knowing which to choose . . . that the perfection of a pure conversational prose-style consists.

And Hazlitt adds: "But in writing a florid and artificial style, neither the same range of invention, nor the same quick sense of propriety—nothing but learning is required." Hazlitt admits to versions of the florid in his own prose; but he recognizes the problem of any style however simple—that, being the product of "research," the difficulty is to preserve plainness. A history of English style might be written by working out what at any given time was meant by "plain" speaking. It is a Shakespearean concern ("Honest plain words best pierce the ear of grief," after the euphuistic fun of *Love's Labour's Lost*). Hazlitt, a stylist with a taste for rhapsody, and a reverence for poetry, considered the problem deeply as it affected the prose writer.

> It has always appeared to me that the most perfect prose-style, the most powerful, the most dazzling, the most daring, that which went nearest to the verge of poetry, and yet never fell over, was Burke's . . . It differs from poetry . . . like the chamois from the eagle: it climbs to an almost equal height, touches upon a cloud, overlooks a precipice, is picturesque, sublime—but all the while, instead of soaring through the air, it stands upon a rocky cliff, clambers up by abrupt and intricate ways, and browzes on the roughest bark, or crops the tender flower.

Hazlitt here allows himself a "poetic" but appropriate illustration of

Burke, metaphorical without being fanciful, a brisk feet-on-the-ground "flight" doing homage to Burke's prose by providing a useful reminder of it. He goes on: "The principle which guides his pen is truth, not beauty— not pleasure, but power." Hazlitt as an essayist was nothing like so constrained as Burke, who "had to treat of political questions, mixed modes, abstract ideas, and his fancy (or poetry, if you will) was ingrafted on these artificially." But Hazlitt as prose writer is always committed to saying what is true, clearly. He is marked off from the poet, however powerfully he brings his "fancy or poetry" into play. Throughout the essays, he is intent on arguing a point, demonstrating a theory, maintaining a belief; "the professed object of prose is to impart conviction." The intellectual activity involved allows little room for merely decorative imagery: "Every word should be a blow: every thought should instantly grapple with its fellow." This interlocking ideal, with the texture of thought and the momentum of discovery, informs the Hazlitt essay. In discussing Milton he indicates clearly the connection between the meaning and music of language. He defends Milton from the charge that because his ideas "were in the highest degree musical" they were not also powerfully descriptive, especially in the main subjects of *Paradise Lost*, "the daring ambition and fierce passions of Satan" and "the paradisaical happiness, and the loss of it" (Hazlitt responds fully to these twin themes of Revolution and Regret). He fully recognizes the power of "the language of music" because of its immediacy. But that "force of style" which is "one of Milton's great excellences" contains other elements. Of the speeches and debates in Pandemonium he notes:

> There is a decided manly tone in the arguments and sentiments,
> an eloquent dogmatism, as if each person spoke from thorough
> conviction; an excellence which Milton probably borrowed from
> his spirit of partisanship . . . That approximation to the severity
> of impassioned prose which has been made an objection to Mil-
> ton's poetry, and which is chiefly to be met with in these bitter
> invectives, is one of its great excellences.

"The severity of impassioned prose," with its fusion of style and conviction, is a Hazlitt ideal. Milton's style is both "musical" and "manly"; Hazlitt, as prose writer and political partisan, naturally admires it. The essayist discovered his "answerable style" in a similar mixture of plain speaking and passion.

Milton's own prose style dissatisfied Hazlitt; it savored "too much of poetry . . . and of an imitation of the Latin." But for Hazlitt ideals of poetry and conversation do not necessarily conflict with regard to prose. He considered Leigh Hunt's prose writing had "the raciness, the sharpness, and sparkling effect of poetry"; if there was also some "relaxation and trifling . . . Still the genuine master-spirit of the prose-writer is there; the tone of lively sensible conversation." Hazlitt's own prose certainly displays this; it also has affinities with Coleridge's development of Cowper's poetry (which Hazlitt admired), the Conversation Poem. The movement from colloquial ease to impassioned meditation, Coleridge's special achievement, likewise informs the Hazlitt essay. Hazlitt of course usually begins with an abstract proposition, and he aims to pursue a course of reasoning—but through a range of mood, in controlled, plain-speaking intimacy.

Hazlitt often returns to the relation of writing and speaking. He cites the opinion of Horne Tooke, that "no one could write a good prose style, who was not accustomed to express himself *viva voce*, or to talk in company." To which Hazlitt responds:

> I certainly so far agree with the above theory as to conceive that no style is worth a farthing that is not calculated to be read out, or that is not allied to spirited conversation; but I at the same time think the process of modulation and inflection may be quite as complete, or more so, without the external enunciation: and that an author had better try the effect of his sentences on his stomach than on his ear. He may be deceived by the last, not by the first.

The ultimate test is an inward one, involving the whole physical being and yet all but silent. He repeats the idea in his essay "On the Conversation of Authors": "there is a method of trying periods on the ear, or weighing them with the scales of the breath, without any articulate sound." And he adds, quoting from his friend J. S. Knowles, "Authors, as they write, may be said to 'hear a sound so fine, there's nothing lives 'twixt it and silence.' Even musicians generally compose in their heads." Hazlitt recognizes that all imaginative language, if it does not aspire to the condition of music, at least approaches musical composition. But he concludes by remarking, "I agree that no style is good, that is not fit to be spoken or read aloud with effect. This holds true not only of emphasis and cadence, but also with regard to natural idiom and colloquial freedom. Sterne's was in this respect the best style that ever was written. You fancy that you hear the people talking." It is a rarer quality than you might think; but in Hazlitt's style too you hear the man talking, a clear energetic voice beautifully informed with common sense, with deep feeling, with conviction.

ROBERT READY

The Logic of Passion: Liber Amoris

No matter what their attitudes toward his involvement with Sarah Walker, most readers of Hazlitt's *Liber Amoris; or, The New Pygmalion* (1823) have been more concerned with the book as biography than they have with the book as literature. Assuming that Hazlitt's only sustained narrative, and one of his longest works, can be viewed critically as well as biographically, I hope to demonstrate the integral position of *Liber Amoris* in Hazlitt's recurrent theme of the sympathetic imagination and to sketch the chief structural and imagistic characteristics of the text.

I

In "On the Spirit of Obligations" (1823), Hazlitt responded to the hostile reception *Liber Amoris* received. "What I would say to any friend who may be disposed to foretel a general outcry against any work of mine, would be to request him to judge and speak of it for himself, as he thinks it deserves." If we accede to this request, by examining *Liber Amoris* within the context of Hazlitt's other writings, we may find it illuminating to determine what connection the work has to the theme many commentators find at the center of the Hazlitt canon. From the time he wrote *An Essay on the Principles of Human Action* (1805), "the natural disinterestedness of the human mind," or the sympathetic imagination, was the fundamental proposition of Hazlitt's thinking and writing. This statement needs multiple qualification beyond the scope of this essay, but essentially, his belief that

From *Studies in Romanticism* 14 (Winter 1975). © 1975 by the Trustees of Boston University. Originally entitled "The Logic of Passion: Hazlitt's *Liber Amoris*."

egoism can and must be transcended by the conjunction of feeling and imagination germinates the convictions and the dramatic tensions of Hazlitt's morality, politics, criticism and familiar essays. "Hazlitt's principle of the sympathetic imagination," writes Ralph Wardle, "is, in fact, the keystone of most of his thinking, political and aesthetic as well as philosophical. For he recognized his own sympathetic imagination as the noblest of his faculties: thanks to it he could *feel with* other human beings, real or fictional."

Liber Amoris is about sympathy in a negative way, a retelling of the Pygmalion legend as a dramatization of an unsympathetic imagination, a lover's attempt to force an earthly girl into the mold of a goddess. The book is Hazlitt's major demonstration of passion blocking the sympathetic perception of an existence separate from one's own.

> H. . . . I would gladly die for you.
> S. That would give me no pleasure. But indeed you greatly overrate my power.
> H. Then that is because you are merciful, and would spare frail mortals who might die with gazing.
> S. I have no power to kill.
> H. . . . if such is thy sweetness where thou dost not love, what must thy love have been? I cannot think how any man, having the heart of one, could go and leave it.
> S. No one did, that I know of.
> H. . . . By Heaven, you are an angel! You look like one at this instant! Do I not adore you—and have I merited this return?
> S. I have repeatedly answered that question. You sit and fancy things out of your own head, and then lay them to my charge.

The modern term "pedestalism" accurately describes H's vision of S. Each time his insistence that she be what he says she is to him crowds her and each time her curt responses guard the little room he leaves her. Often enough she tells him to come down, or at least to let her come down from on high. When he says, "Thou are to me more than thy whole sex," she replies straight enough, "I require no such sacrifices." *Liber Amoris*, then, is a record of what Hazlitt knows to be a most basic human failing— the inability to allow a person to be other than what we want her (or him) to be.

Benjamin Robert Haydon wrote to Mary Russell Mitford that Hazlitt meant "with certain arrangements" to publish his conversations with Sarah Walker and his letters to P. G. Patmore "as a tale of character." Given H's bitter "a more complete experiment on character was never made," the tale may seem to be the woman's, yet the sheer preponderance of H's dialogue and first-person narration shows the focus to be on the man. Intellectually, Hazlitt had long rued the sight of a man trapping himself in his own fixed ideas. In an aside to "Mr. Kean's Iago" (1814), he wrote of those "whose romantic generosity and delicacy ought not to be sacrificed to the baseness of their nature, but who treading securely the flowery path, marked out for them by poets and moralists, the licensed artificers of fraud and lies, are dashed to pieces down the precipice, and perish without help." How ideals of love can become obsessive is explained in an essay of the following year. "Mind and Motive" (1815) argues against self-interest as the dominant principle of action by citing instances of self-destructive behavior. John Kinnaird has demonstrated in what way Hazlitt's theory of the natural benevolence of the mind was finally matched by his realization that the mind can just as naturally sympathize with "power," that is, with an act not conducive to its own or another's good. In "Mind and Motive" Hazlitt writes, "The two most predominant principles in the mind, besides sensibility and self-interest, are imagination and self-will, or (in general) the love of strong excitement, both in thought and action." He continues: "The attention which the mind gives to its ideas is not always owing to the gratification derived from them, but to the strength and truth of the impressions themselves, *i.e.*, to their involuntary power over the mind. This observation will account for a very general principle in the mind, which cannot, we conceive, be satisfactorily explained in any other way, we mean *the power of fascination*." As an instance of the involuntary power of imagination, Hazlitt cites "the necessity which lovers have for confidants, auricular confession," and he concludes: "There are a thousand passions and fancies that thwart our purposes and disturb our repose . . . they assimilate all objects to the gloom of our own thoughts, and make the will a party against itself. This is one chief source of most of the passions that prey like vultures on the heart, and embitter human life." We see that long before he met Sarah Walker, Hazlitt planted a warning before the "flowery path" and gave evidence that imagination can veer into destructive passion.

Even at the time of Hazlitt's intense misery over Sarah Walker, he occasionally shows a double perspective on what was happening to him. "On the Conduct of Life," written in February, 1822, in Scotland, shows him in a black mood, but more importantly it shows him observing the irrational self-laceration of his obsession. He advises his son, to whom this essay is addressed, to choose a woman carefully in order to avoid ridicule and a lack of understanding and sympathy: "We trifle with, make sport of, and despise those who are attached to us, and follow those that fly from us. 'We hunt the wind, we worship a statue, cry aloud to the desert.' " The quotation, varied from Ambrosio's eulogy for the shepherd Chrysostom in *Don Quixote*, functions ironically if we remember Marcela's plea that she is not responsible for the self-destructive passion of Chrysostom. In a stylized passage that he later suppressed from "On the Conduct of Life," Hazlitt warns his son not to "let your blood stagnate in some deep metaphysical question, or refine too much in your ideas of the sex, forgetting yourself in a dream of exalted perfection."

The literary significance, however, of the "book of love" Hazlitt formed out of his dream of Sarah Walker emerges in part from its kinship with some of the literary subjects of the time. P. P. Howe states that *Liber Amoris* is Hazlitt's "*Werther* or *Nouvelle Héloise*." The influence of these recognizable antecedents on Hazlitt ought not shift attention away from the distinct nature of *Liber Amoris* as a work concerning imaginative projection in love. This theme places *Liber Amoris* in a tradition of writing that emerges distinctly in Hazlitt's own period and becomes particularly central to twentieth-century works. Thus in England, *Liber Amoris* suggests the Romantic preoccupation with a certain figure of woman which produced Blake's "Tirzah," Coleridge's "Lewti" and "Christabel," and Keats's "Lamia" and "La Belle Dame." In France Benjamin Constant published *Adolphe* in 1816, a work that also makes structural use of the device of an "editor" publishing the manuscript of a love affair of a man now dead. It has also been noted that Stendhal and Hazlitt had some correspondence prior to this period, that Stendhal's *De l'amour* appeared in 1822 and that Stendhal's theory of crystallization, by which one projects attributes onto one's beloved, finds perfect embodiment in *Liber Amoris*. It is doubtful, though, that Hazlitt knew *De l'amour* at this time, and he did not really come to know Stendhal until the two met in 1824. A review of *De l'amour* did appear in the *New Monthly Magazine* at the end of 1822 (the same magazine in which Hazlitt's "On Great and Little Things" appeared in 1822, an essay which is a notable example of crystallization in its long reference to Sarah Walker). Hazlitt could have read this skeptical review that summarized Stendhal's theory of crystallization and the progressive stages of love. The review ended by exhorting "M. Beyle" to flesh out his theory in a novel.

Like *De l'amour*, *Liber Amoris* should be read as one of the earliest studies of the projective psychology of love. I use the word "study" advisedly, because obviously Hazlitt did not discover the literary material inherent in the projective psychology of love. That material is as old as the Pygmalion legend itself, and one could trace Pygmalion motifs through all of love literature. But as a "tale of character," an extensive treatment of the particular trouble the lover's imagination gets him into, *Liber Amoris* previews a twentieth-century interest in the phenomenon.

To read Thomas Hardy's *The Well-Beloved: A Sketch of a Temperament* (1897) is to find the closest literary analogue to Hazlitt's book; both delineate temperaments that try to duplicate their experience in art with intractable human material. Three other writers should be mentioned: Proust, whose narrator projects his youthful love fantasies onto Gilberte and whose character Swann forges an unlikely idol from Odette; Yeats, who frequently employs themes similar to Hazlitt's Pygmalion theme in such poems as "The Hero, the Girl and the Fool," "The Statues," "The Mask," "Towards Break of Day," "The Grey Rock," "A Memory of Youth," "On Woman," "Broken Dreams," "The "The Tower" (Part II), "Among School Children," and "The Living Beauty"; and Sartre, whose overview of the futility of the love enterprise is that love is perpetual conflict, ultimately an imposibility, since the ideal of both lovers is the appropriation of the beloved's "freedom" or "subjectivity" (*Being and Nothingness*, "Concrete Relations with Others," Section I). Finally, we are not very far away from Jung's concept of the anima when we find Hazlitt writing in "On Great and Little Things" (1822), "The image of some fair creature is engraven on my inmost soul," and in "On the Knowledge of Character" (1821): "The idol we fall down and worship is an image familiar to our minds. It has been present to our waking thoughts, it has haunted us in our dreams, like some fairy vision."

I doubt that *Liber Amoris* was read by any of these other writers; nor is my point to read these writers back into Hazlitt. Yet to go on reading *Liber Amoris* as if it served only Hazlitt's personal ends of confession or catharsis is to tear it out of its proper literary perspective and to treat it as a freak. The frequency with which modern writers have turned to the subject of love's projective psychology shows that *Liber Amoris* anticipates later works as much as it looks to Rousseau and Goethe. It is one of the first extended treatments in a line of modern writing on men who try to make women fit their illusions. In this modern line, Hazlitt's special perspective is that love's projective imagination is an unsympathetic imagination. He does not subtitle his book "The New Pygmalion" without irony. Hazlitt and his character H are the "new" Pygmalions in that Pygmalion's statue was given breath and life, whereas the new Pygmalions have to learn so painfully that their beloveds already have a life and breath of their own.

II

W. E. Henley remarked that *Liber Amoris* "is unique in English." The anonymous *Examiner* critic of a hundred years previous had written: "*Liber Amoris* is a novelty in the English language." "Q." bore down precisely when he summarized the book as the tale of a "highly gifted individual, who having suited himself with a train of very tasteful and elegant associations in relation to female beauty, perfection, and sentiment, is led by a few casual coincidences to infer a perfect adaptation, where nothing of the kind existed." *Liber Amoris* moves on a train of association, and much of the book's great uniqueness, its novelty, results from this movement. We may characterize the structure of Hazlitt's book from his understanding of the associative logic of passion.

Writing of Shakespeare, Hazlitt says that "the greatest strength of genius is shewn in describing the strongest passions." Shakespeare's descriptions of the strongest passions, as in *Cymbeline*, work by "the force of natural association, a particular train of thought suggesting different inflections of the same predominant feeling, melting into, and strengthening one another, like chords in music." *Liber Amoris*, the product of Hazlitt's strongest passion, works in this manner. It is the manner of what Hazlitt calls, in his essay on *King Lear*, "the logic of passion": "We see the ebb and flow of the feeling, its pauses and feverish starts, its impatience of opposition, its accumulating force when it has time to recollect itself, the manner in which it avails itself of every passing word or gesture, its haste to repel insinuation, the alternate contraction and dilatation of the soul."

For Hazlitt, Shakespeare is the very model of the sympathetic imagination. Shakespeare's plays embody the logic of passion because Shakespeare has sympathized with the ebb and flow, the fits and starts of passion. The passion in *Liber Amoris* is the passion of an unsympathetic imagination, the obsession of a lover who refuses to accept a woman as she is. It takes sympathy to follow the logic of this obsession and to recreate that logic in a literary structure. Hazlitt the artist sympathizes with the associative logic of H's unsympathetic passion. The result is the particular structure of *Liber Amoris*.

Hazlitt presents the logic of H's passion in three parts, each of which offers a different perspective on character and action. The work does not have a linear structure. Its progression is a series of movements backward and forward. One result of this kind of progression is a number of shifts in the base line of time, that is, in the time of the narrator in each of the book's three sections.

In the fourth conversation of Part I, we learn that S has been rejected by a previous lover. The fifth scene doubles back in time to depict the first time S told of this rejection. This scene not only precedes the fourth chronologically, but also the second scene. For in the fifth scene, S says that "he is one to whom I feel the sincerest affection, and ever shall, though he is far distant." In the second scene H imagines himself in Italy: "Ah! dearest creature, I shall be 'far distant from you,' as you once said of another, but you will not think of me as of him, 'with the sincerest affection.' " This shift in time points out that the associative logic of passion remembers conversations according to their importance in the development of the relationship rather than their order in time. Short and honed-down, the scenes of Part I enrich one another, but they are without sequence, except for the last two.

The time when the beginning letters of Part II are written overlaps with the time when the final conversations of Part I are written. In the first letter of Part II, H tells C. P., "I have begun a book of our conversations" and he describes the quarrel that made up the penultimate conversation of Part I. Since we are then to think of H's letters in Part II as beginning a good deal before most of the conversations took shape, the result is that the process of writing *Liber Amoris* becomes part of the dramatic action. The base line in time of Part II overtakes Part I when Letter III of Part I reports that the conversations have been finished.

Time displacement avoids straight linear narration in favor of a fragmented or angular presentation of a shattering experience. Since no one perspective sees multiple angles of the experience, Hazlitt forces our perception of character and action to fragment. We must supply our own continuity. (Thus, Letter VI of Part II is written on a steamboat going back to Scotland; that H has returned to London and thrown a violent scene goes quite unexplained until Part III.) The continuity Hazlitt constructs is psychological rather than narrative; it is the continuity of the logic of passion in H's associating mind as he remembers and writes.

This associating mind, to return to the incisive remark of the *Examiner* reviewer, is that of "a highly gifted individual," who has "suited himself with a train of very tasteful and elegant associations in relation to female beauty, perfection, and sentiment." Hazlitt has significantly altered his own personality in creating H. Not only, for example, has he edited out the obscenities in his original letters to Patmore, but he has also given a good deal more coherence to some of the disconnected ravings we find in the original letters. The cooler, more even H who results from this revision is indeed a tasteful, elegant and highly gifted individual. Hazlitt's character is a man who often perceives life through the mediation of art. He continually thinks in terms of previous literature, of writer, and of images both plastic and literary.

The first conversation, a microcosm of the whole, demonstrates the complex mediation by which H transforms S. "The Picture" immediately allies with the Pygmalion motif. H shows S a miniature by Raphael.

> H. Don't you think it like yourself?
> S. No: it's much handsomer than I can pretend to be.
> H. That's because you don't see yourself with the same eyes
>   that others do.

She changes the subject, asking what the picture is. He replies: "Some say it is a Madona [*sic*]; others call it a Magdalen, and say you may distinguish the tear upon the cheek, though no tear is there. But it seems to me more like Raphael's St. Cecilia, 'with looks commercing with the skies,' than anything else."

His reply is packed. By being associated with the patron saint of music, S now belongs to its harmony, and the other dialogues sometimes speak of her in terms of music. H's own St. Cecilia also has " 'looks commercing with the skies,' " that is, her harmony bridges to higher harmony, perhaps the music of the spheres. The quotation is line 39 of Milton's *Il Penseroso*, where the poet addresses Melancholy, the "pensive Nun, devout and pure" (l. 31). S's reticence may suggest melancholy; but following immediately after the Cecilia reference, the quotation, by evoking *Il Penseroso* re-enforces the high seriousness of H's vision of S. Furthermore, H seems to refer to the whole passage from Milton:

> Com, but keep thy wonted state,
> With eev'n step and musing gate,
> And looks commercing with the skies,
> Thy rapt soul sitting in thine eyes:
> There held in holy passion still,
> Forget thy self to Marble, till
> With a sad Leaden downward cast,
> Thou fix them on the earth as fast.
>
> (ll. 37–44)

Liber Amoris makes a good deal of S's graceful manner of walking and the singular expression of her eyes. It persistently uses "marble" to describe her, sometimes adoringly, sometimes bitterly. And of course, something akin to "holy passion" is attributed to her several times. Also, as this conversation ends, H speaks of "your mouth full of suppressed sensibility, your downcast eyes, the soft blush upon that cheek." The features he sees could well be those of the "pensive Nun, devout and pure," and S's "downcast eyes" recall specifically line 43 of the poem (with perhaps another echo, Spenser's "Epithalamion," l. 234, "her eyes still fastened on the ground").

In addition to this Miltonic mode, other literary references abound in *Liber Amoris*. H is Aeneas: "But even in another world, I suppose you would turn from me" (see *The Aeneid*, Book VI 469–473). He sarcastically refers her to the Carthaginian wars: "Hers is the Fabian method of making love and conquests." As he returns to Scotland on "a sort of spectre-ship, moving on through an infernal lake, without wind or tide, by some necromantic power," like the Mariner he feels "the eternity of punishment in this life"; and, like the Coleridge of "Dejection: An Ode," he has "conversed too long with abstracted truth." One has, in fact, only to glance at Howe's notes to see the fabric H weaves out of literary and mythological references throughout *Liber Amoris*. "Those lines in Tibullus seem to have been written on purpose for her. . . . Or what do you think of those in a modern play, which might actually have been composed with an eye to this little trifler—." When he asks S's sister to convey three books to S "in lieu of three volumes of my own writings" and the young girl replies, " 'AND THOSE ARE THE ONES THAT SHE PRIZES THE MOST!' " {*sic*}, H swells into "If there were ever words spoken that could revive the dead." This almost hyper-literary sensibility, so imbued with quotations that give substance to his unreciprocated love, and so betokened by the physical presence of books themselves, has only to be equipped with several passages relating his communion with or disjunction from the picturesque and sublime in nature, to create the complete man of feeling who projects the world from his own center and whose fallacies are truly pathetic.

Literary references, the overlay of nature topoi familiar from the literature of the time, books, and the reader's unbroken awareness of the process of this epistolary work are further reinforced by a complex system of image and symbol. The overall illusion-reality theme is elaborated in imagery of two main types: what I will term a lamia group (such as serpent, poison, witch, enchantress) and a Pygmalion group (such as statue, picture, marble, stone). There are also brief but important instances of flower and weed images. Hazlitt's complex uses of imagery flow naturally from the sub-title, "The New Pygmalion." The associative logic of H's passion continually works changes on a set body of images. I will first sketch the movement of the imagery in Parts I and II in order to devote space to imagery in the climactic Part III.

The fourth conversation, "The Flageolet," first develops the Pygmalion motif: "Cruel girl! you . . . resemble some graceful marble statue. . . . I could worship you at this moment." He reverses the motif in an important pre-figuring of a crisis point in Part III: "You see you can mould me as you like." The sixth conversation, "The Quarrel," concludes by introducing the imagery which Hazlitt later inverts to close *Liber Amoris*: "Thou wert to me a little tender flower, blooming in the wilderness of my life; and though thou should'st turn out a week, I'll not fling thee from me, while I can help it." He then entreats her, "Kiss me, thou little sorceress!" As the conversations began about a picture, they end focusing on a statue, when H asks if he resembles her old lover:

> S. No, Sir. . . . But there was a likeness.
> H. To whom?
> S. To that little image! (*looking intently on a small bronze figure of Buonaparte on the mantelpiece*).

The Pygmalion theme is now complete; they both have their images. H's final gloss ironically counterpoints the theme: "[And then I added 'How odd it was that the God of my idolatry should turn out to be like her Idol, and said it was no wonder that the same face which awed the world should conquer the sweetest creature in it!']." Part I ends with two letters followed by a note "Written in a blank leaf of Endymion" (presumably Keats's); he wishes for the picture "to kiss and talk to" and begs pardon for the quarrel: "I hope the *little image* made it up between us &c." That the note is written in a blank leaf of *Endymion* allies H with the prototype of a man who falls in love with an ideal woman. And the note may also have further connection with Keats' *Lamia* volume (1820): "—But by her dove's eyes and serpent-shape, I think she does not hate me; by her smooth forehead and her crested hair, I own I love her; by her soft looks and queen-like grace (which men might fall down and worship) I swear to live and die for her!."

In Letter I of Part II, H tells C. P., "I have begun a book of our conversations (I mean mine and the statue's . . .)." H recounts the quarrel swiftly, prefaced by "She cajoled me out of my little Buonaparte as cleverly as possible," and concluding with "So I must come back for it." H encloses the first of the two letters to S that ended Part I; he remarks that the letter "might move a stone." Letter II encloses her frigid reply and begins to dress his fears and imaginings. He is of two minds about her: "I suspect her

grievously of being an arrant jilt, to say no more—yet I love her dearly."
His role as cynical lover is contained in the phrase "before you set about
your exposition of the new Apocalypse of the new Calypso," certainly a facile
remark but in line with the enchantress-witch complex. He goes on to relate
additional conversations, but he now remembers her remarks as non-sequiturs
or as coy and ambiguous: "After all, what is there in her but a pretty figure,
and that you can't get a word out of her."

Despair in the third letter intensifies the "arrant jilt" suspicion through
the lamia imagery: "If I knew she was a mere abandoned creature, I should
try to forget her; but till I do know this, nothing can tear me from her, I
have drank in poison from her lips too long—alas! mind do not poison
again." Reassured in Letter IV that S is chaste, H raises the Pygmalion strain:
"my heart's idol . . . the dear saint . . . the sweet apparition." This relative
altitude continues in Letter V as H launches into her praise: "I could devour
the little witch. If she had plague-spot on her, I could touch the infection:
if she was in a burning fever, I could kiss her, and drink death as I have
drank life from her lips. . . . It is not what she says or what she does—it
is herself that I love." The morbid imagery recurs from "The Quarrel,"
where H exclaimed, "wert thou a wretched wanderer in the street, covered
with rags, disease, and infamy, I'd clasp thee to my bosom, and live and
die with thee, my love." In Letter VI, the Buonaparte statue symbolizes S's
old lover: she "only played with my credulity till she could find some one
to supply the place of her unalterable attachment to *the little image*." His
own Pygmalion sickness worsens as he writes, "I cannot forget *her*; and I
can find no other like what *she seemed*," and as he closes by asking P to see
if any reconciliation is possible or if she is "quite marble." Disaffected from
nature in Letter VIII—"The sky is marble to my thoughts"—an inanimate
figure haunts him: "I wake with her by my side, not as my sweet bedfellow,
but as the corpse of my love. . . ." An apostrophe following Letter VIII
recasts the theme of the inanimate: " 'Stony-hearted' Edinburgh! What are
thou to me? . . . City of palaces, or of tombs—a quarry, rather than the
habitation of men! . . . Thy cold grey walls reflect back the leaden melancholy of the soul." Thus divorce from both nature and city is expressed
in terms of inanimate substance. The logic of passion, through its preoccupation with the hard, unresponsive beloved, links all other things in a
chain of similar images.

In Letter IX, H distances himself sufficiently to ponder the illusion/
reality split: "fancying a little artful vixen to be an angel and a saint"; "my
life (that might have been so happy, had she been what I thought her)";
"For this picture, this ecstatic vision, what have I of late instead as the

image of the reality?" The lamia returns: "I see the young witch seated in another's lap, twining her serpent arms round him, her eye glancing and her cheeks on fire." Even so, he plans still to offer marriage and begs that his letter be seen as "the picture of a half-disordered mind." A descriptive passage in Letter X then recasts familiar images: "the river winded its dull, slimy way like a snake along the marshy grounds: and the dim misty tops of Ben Leddi, and the lovely Highlands (woven fantastically of thin air) mocked my embraces and tempted my longing eyes like her, the sole queen and mistress of my thoughts!" Once more, by relating images he has employed for S with images in nature, H expresses the associative psychology of passion. Nature fuses the morbid and the inanimate into a climactic death fantasy: "As I trod the green mountain turf, oh! how I wished to be laid beneath it—in one grave with her—that I might sleep with her in that cold bed, my hand in hers, and my heart for ever still—while worms should taste her sweet body, that I had never tasted!"

Letter XI oscillates, as did Letter IX, between hard-hitting analysis of S and dejection at her loss. S is the "well practiced illusion,' while H writes of himself, "abased and brutalised as I have been by that Circean cup of kisses, of enchantments, of which I have drunk!" The last mythological reference was to Calypso in Letter II. Choice of witch figures intensifies with H's changing mind about S. The flip reference to Calypso gives way to Circe, whose enchantment was vicious and lethal. Short and business-like, Letter XII directs P to tell M, S's brother-in-law, that H will propose marriage. This letter is followed by pieces entitled "Unaltered Love" and "Perfect Love." The former shows that H is, in a major respect, exactly where he started: "I will make a Goddess of her, and build a temple to her in my heart, and worship her on indestructible altars, and raise statues to her." "From C. P., Esq." then relates the outcome of P's visit to M, to the effect that H ought to come back and propose. Letter XIII is jubilant: "She is an angel from Heaven, and you cannot pretend I ever said a word to the contrary!" He has seen a painting (*Hope Finding Fortune in the Sea*) whose female figure mirrored S—"If it is not the very image of her, I am no judge." With the picture motif returns the statue motif: "I have had her face constantly before me, looking so like some faultless marble statue, as cold, as fixed and graceful as ever statue did."

Part III is a self-contained narrative of events between H's sudden visit to London through the final break with S: he returns to London, throws a violent scene following the most distancing reception from S, returns to Scotland until his divorce is finalized, comes back only to see S in the street one day with another man. Part III concludes with H's analysis of her character.

He begins, "My dear K—, It is all over, and I know my fate." Physical motion is also fated in Part III, as a kind of enchantment or magnetism seems to control H, forcing him to play out the drama almost unwittingly. When S is "frank and cordial" to him for the first time—"This of course acted as a spell on me." He goes out with his son, but "I found that I still contrived to bend my steps towards her, and I went back to take tea." There follows a maddening interview with S; he snaps, and screams out his anguish. Again he tries to get away and again he is riveted back: "I was no sooner in the street, than the desolation and the darkness became greater, more intolerable; and the eddying violence of my passion drove me back to the source, from whence it sprung." These two motions out and back anticipate the book's climax, where motion is choreographed, the figures encountering one another as if in a passing dream:

> I passed a house in King Street where I had once lived, and had not proceeded many paces, ruminating on chance and change and old times, when I saw her coming towards me. I felt a strange pang at the sight, but I thought her alone. Some people before me moved on, and I saw another person with her. *The murder was out.* . . . We passed at the crossing of the street without speaking. . . . I turned and looked—they also turned and looked—and as if by mutual consent, we both retrod our steps and passed again, in the same way. I went home. I was stifled.

After so long in his obsessive maze, the way out comes simply, and the effect is masterful. The two previous movements have solidified its power.

Hazlitt maintains an increasingly symbolic use of the Buonaparte statue before the King Street climax. When H first returns from Scotland, he finds the statue back on his mantelpiece, which he considers "a sort of recognition of old times." He spins the fact that she has kept it into new hope, and the evening when he breaks loose in rage begins as he tries to get S to sit and talk with him. When she refuses, he says, " 'Well, then, for the sake of *the little image!'* The appeal seemed to have lost its efficacy; the charm was broken; she remained immoveable." After she leaves, he rails hysterically, and grabbing the statue, smashes it to pieces. The next day he picks up the pieces and sends them contritely to S. He tries to bring the next conversation around to sentimental matters, but she puts him off: " 'I was sadly afraid the *little image* was dethroned from her heart, as I had dashed it to the ground the other night.'—'She was neither desperate nor violent.' " Upon his return from Scotland, he asks her to get the statue repaired. Within a few days her mother tells him that S is out doing just that: "My heart, my poor fond heart, almost melted within me at this news." The next morning she returns with the statue whole again. They shake hands in reconciliation, "and she went waving out of the room." This is the day before King Street, after which we hear no more of the statue, except for one contemptuous reference to the "*little image*" so suddenly displaced from her breast by the new suitor.

Hazlitt continues to orchestrate the other image clusters through Part III. As they first speak of the Buonaparte again: "Her words are few and simple; but you can have no idea of the exquisite, unstudied, irresistible graces with which she accompanies them, unless you can suppose a Greek statue to smile, move, and speak." Poison and death: "I had drank in the poison of her sweetness too long ever to be cured of it; and though I might find it to be poison in the end, it was still in my veins. My only ambition was to be permitted to live with her, and to die in her arms." His fantasy of picking her off the street returns: "I felt that my soul was wedded to hers; and were she a mere lost creature, I would try to snatch her from perdition."

Through Part III, H continues thinking of S in the Pygmalion terms. When he asks her to get the Buonaparte fixed, he marvels at her face, the "finest expression that ever was seen . . . but without speaking a word, without altering a feature. It was like a petrifaction of a human face in the softest moment of passion." Before King Street she is his "earthly Goddess"; afterwards he sees only a "pale cold form" and a "lifeless image." Life has finally left Pygmalion's substance.

The most climactic use of imagery in Part III merges the lamia and Pygmalion groups shortly before the King Street denouement:

> It was a fable. She started up in her own likeness, a serpent in place of a woman. She had fascinated, she had stung me, and had returned to her proper shape, gliding from me after inflicting the mortal wound, and instilling deadly poison into every pore; but her form lost none of its original brightness by the change of character, but was all glittering, beauteous, voluptuous grace. Seed of the serpent or of the woman, she was divine! I felt that she was a witch, and had bewitched me. Fate had enclosed me round about. *I* was transformed too, no longer human (any more than she, to whom I had knit myself) my feelings were marble; my blood was of molten lead; my thoughts on fire. I was taken out of myself, wrapt into another sphere, far from the light of day, of hope, of love. I had no natural affection left; she had slain me, but no other thing had power over me.

We saw the reverse Pygmalion theme briefly in Part I, "The Flageolet."

Here in Part III, the metamorphosis of the artist is complete. Hazlitt also ends his book by reversing the flower-weed imagery of "The Quarrel": "Her image seems fast 'going into the wastes of time,' like a weed that the wave bears farther and farther from me. Alas! thou poor hapless weed, when I entirely lose sight of thee, and for ever, no flower will ever bloom on earth to glad my heart again!"

At the end H sees the whole affair as a "frightful illusion." And though, as the final long indictment of S shows, he does not blame himself, he does discern that she resented his vision: "She in fact knows what she is, and recoils from the good opinion or sympathy of others, which she feels to be founded on a deception; so that my over-weening opinion of her must have appeared like irony, or direct insult." As difficult as it is for him to believe other than that "she still *is* what she so long *seemed*," he will not relinquish the original vision for having been tricked and deluded by it. Tortured, he is far from broken, and confesses nothing. The anima, if you will, remains: "I know all this; but what do I gain by it, unless I could find some one with her shape and air, to supply the place of the lovely apparition?"

We may infer that as long as H longs for apparitions he will fail to see real existences. Hazlitt's "tale of character" tells how what is protects itself against what one would have. Wrenched out of his own worst years to be a negative example in his pervasive concern with the practical and aesthetic value of sympathy, *Liber Amoris* articulated the logic of passion and dramatized that no person can successfully appropriate the being of another. Hazlitt spoke from experience in "On Personal Identity" (1828) when he wrote that despite a man's high intentions, a woman resents being insistently thought of as something she is not. "We are not," the essay concludes, "to be cozened out of our existence for nothing."

JOHN KINNAIRD

The Modern Difference:
Comedy and the Novel

"Joys laugh not! Sorrows weep not!" Blake's proverb was certainly true of the Romantic age, which found tranquillity of spirit in contemplating the still, sad music of humanity and was seldom more solemn or melancholy than when it spoke of Joy. Byron remembered a Methodist preacher shouting in the direction of some profane grins, "No *hopes* for them as *laughs!*"—and this warning of grave spiritual dangers in laughter found an echo in a contemporary of another faith, the young Shelley, whose hopes for mankind similarly moved him to deplore "the withering and perverting spirit of comedy." There was still, of course, plenty of convivial laughter in Regency England, but wit and humor were increasingly constrained, at least when removed from the arena of politics, to be morally circumspect and "amiable." The professional jesters of the age—Lamb, Peacock, Sydney Smith—were masters of the art of keeping their shafts of satire inoffensively light and were ready at a moment's notice to modulate their humor into earnest doctrine or serious sentiment—the one inconsistent exception to this rule being the defiant author of *Don Juan*. Nor did Hazlitt, with his own sacred pieties to defend, escape the prevailing conspiracy against Momus. Leigh Hunt tells the story of being in company with Hazlitt and Lamb one evening when the conversation turned to a line in a poem of Marvell's, describing a tidal flood in the Netherlands, where the fish were said to have come swimming up to Dutch dinner tables "And sat not as a meat, but as a guest." Hazlitt insisted to his friends that this "forced, far-fetched" conceit was not the least bit funny; and he was about to launch "into a very acute

From *William Hazlitt: Critic of Power*. © 1978 by Columbia University Press.

discourse to prove that we ought *not to laugh* at such exaggerations, when we were forced to interrupt him by a fit of laughter uncontrollable."

A certain resistance to risibility may be, however, more of an asset than a liability for the critic of comedy. Hazlitt's distrust of wit does breed difficulties for his theory of comedy, but the fact is that he is never consistently better as a descriptive critic, never more at ease with his materials, than in *Lectures on the English Comic Writers* (1819). Whenever Hazlitt pauses in his theory to give vent to his moral suspicion of wit, we may recognize again the voice of his priggish Unitarian conscience; and the same voice may be heard more ambivalently in his protestation that his temperament is, to a fault, "more saturnine than mercurial" and that he possesses not "a grain of wit." The first statement may be true enough of Hazlitt the man, but the latter is by no means true of the writer, as not a few quotations in this study will attest. Hazlitt had inherited a good deal of his father's "monkish pleasantry," and although in the son that humor was more deeply fused with the Hazlitt earnestness, the fusion made for a happy balance of values in his criticism—insuring both a congenial response to, and a deliberate judgment of, the ways of comic genius. Of the intimate nexus between the comic sense of irony and his critical faculties, Hazlitt was keenly aware: the poets of the *Lyrical Ballads*, he once observed, would never say that "I got my liking for the novelists or the comic writers . . . from them. If so, I must have got from them what they never had themselves. . . . In forming an estimate of passages relating to common life and manners, I cannot think I am a plagiarist from any man."

Hazlitt knew, moreover, that the paradox of a saturnine man secretly in love with laughter was no anomaly in England. When Hunt described his friend as a man with a strong sense of humor but without "animal spirits enough" to revel in merriment, he was really describing what Hazlitt would have recognized as a familiar variant of the English character. English "mirth," he observes in his essay "Merry England," is "a relaxation from gravity"; a jest is welcomed as "a streak of light" athwart "our natural gloom." Among the French or Italians too lively "a pitch of animal spirits runs away with the imagination" and tempts the mind to "take a jest for granted"; but "the ludicrous takes hold" of an Englishman's mind from the very "hardness and repulsiveness" of his feelings, which are "not easily reconciled" to an equivalent "obtuseness" in the minds or bodies of other Englishmen. Hazlitt might have added to this account that the very word *humor*, in its modern and pleasurable sense as applied to character and expression in comedy, is an English invention. As Stuart M. Tave has shown, a long and gradual revolution in English comic theory had "essentially reversed" the original meaning of "humour" as a willful or knavish aberration to be exposed and mocked out of existence (or into humility) by the critical genius of "wit." Hazlitt's sense of his own credentials for criticism of comedy exhibits this new tolerance for the eccentric; both the lecturer and his audience were prepared to find the greatest pleasure of comedy, not in deft ridicule of fools and rogues, but in those amiable and picturesque "originals" of quirky humanity—a Falstaff, a Don Quixote, an Uncle Toby—who bear witness to the comic genius of Nature herself.

Yet just as there is more acidulous wit in Hazlitt's intelligence than he cares to admit, so more of the Augustan conception of "wit" survives in his theory of the comic than his Romantic predilection for the greater humaneness of "humour" would suggest. Hazlitt formulates three main types of comedy, which he correlates with three phases in the development of English comedy, and also with—though he does not obtrude the connection upon his audience—three "degrees of the laughable" described in the opening lecture, "On Wit and Humour." The first phase, and most elementary type, is "comedy of nature," found at its purest in Shakespeare and his age; this type is succeeded by "comedy of manners" or "artificial comedy," which has its greatest flowering in the Restoration and which Hazlitt is to praise as the "highest" comedy; and this in turn is followed by the "sentimental comedy" of the eighteenth century and of his own time, which for Hazlitt is not properly comedy at all, since it retains only the forms of comic drama without its essence. What differentiates the three phases as types is their way of combining—or, in the latter case, of failing to combine—the "degrees" of laughter: the "merely laughable," the "ludicrous," and the "ridiculous." The first degree, present in all comic incident, is laughter provoked by simple surprise and contrast—by some sudden "disconnection" between expectation and event, an incongruity which in itself may be meaningless, mere "accident." Laughter on this level is therefore not properly comic until it coincides with the second degree, the "ludicrous." Here laughter is sustained by a further incongruity in character or situation, so that the surprising event does not merely startle by its oddity but contradicts our sense of "what is customary or desirable," yet is still not so shocking or offensive as to be noticeably unpleasant. This is the basis for "comedy of nature," whose ruling principle is "humour," or "the describing the ludicrous as it is in itself" (that is, without express or implied comparison with something else). Only incidentally does this mode of comedy attain to the "ridiculous," which is the forte of "artificial comedy." This type is characteristic of a more advanced stage of society, when the laughable arises less from incongruities "of nature and accident" than from something "which is contrary . . . to sense and reason, or is a voluntary departure from what we have a right to expect from those who are conscious of absurdity and propriety in words, looks, and actions." Here the sense of the incongruous finds expression, as in Restoration manners comedy, in satiric "wit," which seeks not merely to present or describe but to mock what is ludicrous by "comparing or contrasting it with something else." As soon as wit succeeds, however, in making vice, vanity, and folly appear ridiculous, a public reaction sets in against the licentious vanities of wit itself; and then the values of moral sentiment overwhelm both wit and humor in "sentimental comedy," which finds more pleasure in the tears of sympathy than in laughter at absurdity. From this sad decline English comedy had not yet recovered—and, Hazlitt feared, would never recover.

This scheme is impressive, and much of it still makes good sense; but as a historical formulation it is, of course, much too logical to be descriptively adequate; it is, indeed, in the most fundamental sense, not historical at all, for it assumes that the major phases in the development of comedy are serially predetermined by a "natural" logic inhering in certain causes and consequences. And as a theoretic description of the comic impulse, the logic of this scheme proves to be less consistent with Hazlitt's own psychology than with the rationalism of the previous century. As various commentators have pointed out, Hazlitt's theory has direct eighteenth-century antecedents: the distinctions on which he bases his "degrees" had at least been adumbrated before; his originality lies mainly in the psychological rationale that he provides for these terms and in applying them to correlative periods in literary history. It is perhaps ironic that a theory which leads to the condemnation of eighteenth-century comedy should have originated in the most characteristic assumptions of that century; for the "incongruity" theory of comic laughter, which descends from Aristotle, ultimately depends on the sentiment of rationalism—on belief in a constant, predictable if not intelligible order in the world. No one would deny that "incongruity" is in some sense indispensable to all comic effect, but to make it the motive of all laughter is to reduce comic pleasure to the status of a neural symptom—the transitory accompaniment to an intellectual act which restores to consciousness the cognitive norms of probability (or, if there is moral judgment as well, of "propriety"). By this theory, people never really *expect* to laugh; and when they do, they laugh only to rid themselves of the anomalous disturbance. "It is astonishing," Hazlitt once remarked, "how much wit and laughter there is in the world . . . and yet, being excited by what is *out of the way* and singular, it ought to be rare and gravity should be the order of the day." To us it may seem more astonishing that a theorist who could entertain this reflection should have lost none of his confidence in the theoretic sufficiency of the incongruity principle.

There are moments in his first lecture when Hazlitt's theorizing seems on the verge of proposing new and sounder premises for comedy, and not the least promising moment comes with his opening statement: "Man is the only animal that laughs and weeps; for he is the only animal that is struck with the difference between what things are, and what they ought to be." The close conjunction here of laughter and tears is further established by some remarks on the behavior of children—observations on their exuberance and "animal spirits," their sheer readiness to laugh, the sudden, sometimes instantaneous transition from laughter to tears and back; on the rhythm of this movement, the "alternate excitement and relaxation of the imagination," which seems itself pleasurable to the child, or not wholly dependent on the discontinuity of appearances which is its exciting cause. Yet these insights, pregnant with new theory, are then abruptly forgotten as Hazlitt proceeds to analyze the "comic" in its contradistinction to the "serious." The latter is defined as "the habitual stress which the mind lays upon the expectation of a given order of events": when this stress or "weight of interest" is increased or "overstrained' by some "violent opposition," the serious mounts into "the pathetic or tragical," but when "abruptly loosened or relaxed," dissolves into the "ludicrous." As long as we keep our focus on the extremes in this contrast, Hazlitt's reasoning seems convincing enough; but we need only consider the intermediate range between these extremes to recognize that comedy and tragedy do not inhabit emotionally alien spheres but respond to the same polarity, partake of the same life-tension in consciousness. One is not more congruent with the nature of things than the other; they are concerned not with a different "opposition" but, in different ways, with the same human predicament—the disparity between reality and desire, actuality and value, things that "are" and "ought to be." The comic in literature, unlike the "laughable" in life, can only be a mode of awareness, not a state of feeling. Literary genres cannot be made to correspond to distinct psychological states, and only in his theory of comedy does Hazlitt's literary theory fall into this error.

Where this theory most obviously betrays its literary inadequacy is in his account of Shakespeare's comedies—although the same lecture (the second, "On Shakespeare and Ben Jonson") provides, as so often happens in Hazlitt, the means, in its incidental insights, for correcting his prejudices. The worst practical consequence of his faulty theory is that it prevents him from arriving at a conception of Shakespearean comedy *as drama*—such a conception as his theory does enable him to bring to the comedy of the

Restoration. The very ability that serves Hazlitt so well in dealing with the tragedies now breeds confusion and distraction; for without the cue of tragic passion, his feeling for character leads him away, rather than toward, the dramatic center of the plays. Whenever character rises above the design, Hazlitt's portraiture (in the essays on the comedies and the histories in *Characters*) is likely to be as telling as ever: his masterpiece in this vein is his full-length, six-page sketch of Falstaff, and so brilliant is this portrait of comic exuberance incarnate ("He manures and nourishes his mind with jests, as he does his body with sack and sugar") that we are likely to overlook the ultimate infidelity of the all-too-amiable figure that Hazlitt creates to Shakespeare's all-too-human Sir John. The trouble here, as in all his commentary on the comedies, is that Hazlitt does not know what to do with the characters after stamping their authenticity; they amuse or entrance him with their "humours," and he assumes that this can be their only meaning in "the comedy of nature." His vision of Shakespeare's comic world is of a riotous paradise of impulse, in which the flora and fauna of almost every known species of human foible and folly "shoot out with native, happy, unchecked luxuriance," while their creator, like a benign English gardener, beams upon them and humors his own fond fancy as he does everything he can to "pamper" their whims.

This vision still has much persuasive force; we have here a primitive version of C. L. Barber's view of Shakespearean comedy as "festive" comedy, "concerned with the relation between man and the nature celebrated by holiday, not relations between social classes and types." But what is clearly wrong in Hazlitt's praise is the judgmental conclusion to which he is pointing: that the comedies, happy and winning though they are, are "deficient," are not "great" as the tragedies are great; again the assumption is that comedy can be great only to the degree that it provokes either satiric or "amiable" laughter—and preferably in that order of frequency. Shakespeare's Muse was "too good-natured and magnanimous"; "we sympathize with his characters oftener than we laugh at them." It was not that Shakespeare lacked talent for comedy ("He had an equal genius for comedy and tragedy"); it was rather that his other gifts overwhelmed his comic powers and prevented their purely comic fruition. "Shakespeare was a greater poet than wit: his imagination was the leading and master-quality of his mind, which was always ready to soar into its native element: the ludicrous was only secondary and subordinate."

What, though, is Hazlitt really saying here? Is he saying that Shakespeare's comedy suffered from an excess of his humor and "fancy" at the expense of wit, or that there is a natural and, sooner or later, exclusive antagonism between comedy and the sympathies of poetic imagination?

Reluctantly, Hazlitt seems to decide for the latter alternative: "I do not, in short, consider comedy as exactly an affair of the heart or the imagination; and it is for this reason only that I think Shakespeare's comedies deficient." But Hazlitt's comparison of Shakespeare with Ben Jonson suggests a different reading. Although the author of *Volpone* clearly transcends this limitation, Jonson's characters are too "mean," his plots too "mechanical"; he has the comic "extravagance" but not the comic exuberance. And how little Hazlitt is willing, in his specific judgments, to separate wit and poetic imagination, whatever his theory may say, is clear from his comment that Jonsonian comedy wants "that genial spirit of enjoyment and finer fancy, which constitutes the essence of poetry and of wit." The "disconnection" of our sympathies which Hazlitt imputes to wit would therefore seem to be more apparent than real, or a reference to the effects of wit on the audience, rather than to its essence or to the process of its creation. Such, at least, seems the most obvious way of reconciling the foregoing with Hazlitt's general conclusions:

> Wit, as distinguished from poetry, is the imagination or fancy inverted, and so applied to given objects, as to make the little look less, the mean more light and worthless; or to divert our admiration or wean our affections from that which is lofty or impressive, instead of producing a more intense admiration and exalted passion, as poetry does.

"Admiration": again that word may help us absolve Hazlitt from confusion. He believes that comedy finds its generic consummation in satire, yet he is unable or unwilling to postulate a clear continuity in imagination between humor and wit; and one reason why he cannot or will not do so is that all the instincts of his upbringing tempt him to conceive of that continuity as moral and historical, rather than "natural"—rather than as a tendency inhering in given values and powers of the mind. Since, we remember, the sympathy of poetic imagination is with "power" as well as value, that "admiration" needs continual chastening; and Hazlitt sees wit, "the eloquence of indifference," as imagination correcting its errors and excesses of "admiration" by "inverting" or "diverting" its sympathies. But the power to do so cannot properly exist in the mind, that is, can have no proper function, until the original sin of "aggrandizing" worldly power beyond its value has actually been committed in the world, and on a scale that thoroughly confuses the motives of power and value in society. This for Hazlitt is the ultimate function of comic genius in the cause of "humanity": not merely to expose and censure, in the Augustan way, the grossness or pettiness of vice and folly, but to challenge and counterbalance the idolatry of power which is latent in all imagination and which even the greatest poetic genius tends in some degree to flatter—witness Shakespeare's in *Coriolanus*. Here we see the role of comic theater, and especially of "comedy of manners," in Hazlitt's myth of "progress" through genius: while the other arts foster pleasure and passional sympathy, comedy converts antipathy to virtue, through farcical exaggeration or merciless ridicule of false power: "I think that comedy does not find its richest harvest till individual infirmities have passed into general manners, and it is the example of courts chiefly [as in the Stuart Restoration], that stamps folly with credit and currency, or glosses over vice with meretricious lustre."

But by this account "wit," and by extension all comic invention which aims at more than "fancy," remains anti-poetic, essentially negative and inhumane, untrue in itself—in a word, purely reactive, dependent for meaning on its emotional contrary and its moral effect, expressing the incongruous only by making it appear more contemptibly absurd. And by this reasoning, too, modern comedy must die when its countervailing delusion in society dies. This is the mythic logic that nominally governs the progression of the *Lectures*, and we shall find that Hazlitt can make much of it sound persuasive, even at this remote distance. He is, however, finally too intelligent, has too much love and respect for the great wits of English literature—and perhaps too much also for his own powers of wit—to let this solemn fiction stand as his final judgment on the "truth" of wit. In "On Wit and Humour" Hazlitt had reaffirmed the Augustan distinction between "true" and "false" wit, but he had done so in very general terms, by likening "true" wit and its powers of "detection'" to acuteness of reasoning or "subtle observation"— a truth of content rather than one inhering in form, in the processes of wit itself; wit is seen as departing from reason, and thus from truth, in its distinctive attraction to "accidental" or "verbal combinations." Not until a late essay, "Definition of Wit" (1829), does Hazlitt return to the question, and there his account of wit, although largely the same, differs in precisely this particular: the metaphoric play of wit is seen now, not as a projection of images and verbal novelties designed to "mock" or "belittle," but as an act of "discursive" imagination, dissolving habitual "aggregates" in the mind and recombining their ideas (as we would say today, condensing and displacing them) so as to reveal otherwise undetected truth, some contradiction or "double meaning" that we would otherwise be unable or unwilling to acknowledge. Rescued at last from the role of playing the jolly or mischievous fool to the king of "lofty" poetry, wit is now defined as "one mode of viewing and representing nature, or the difference and similitudes, the harmonies and discords in the links and chains of our ideas of things at large."

Characteristically, Hazlitt admits to no disparity between the two accounts of wit. yet, in another sense, he was right not to do so, for most of his 1819 *Lectures*, or at least those dealing with the Restoration and the comic tradition thereafter, do faithfully present a vision of "truth" as inhering either in the comedic form itself or in the historically dynamic relationship of a changing form with a changing subject matter. And nowhere does this enlarged vision of the comic emerge more strongly than in Hazlitt's unprecedented account of the novel and of its enormous potential for greatness as a form. We recall, at the start of this chapter, Hazlitt defending the originality of his comic sense "in forming an estimate of passages relating to common life and manners." It is this change of direction emerging in the later lectures—a change from comedy in its classical function as a "test" of truth by ridicule to comic "truth" as having its own substantial existence in the processes of experience, a sense of "truth" which anticipates also many of the attitudes known to a later generation as *realism*—that will prove most important to trace here for our purposes, as it signals a major shift in Hazlitt's understanding of what is "modern" in literature and in life.

Among the major English critics Hazlitt stands alone in his unstinting praise of the Restoration as "the golden period of our comedy." All that had glittered treacherously in the reigns of the later Stuart kings became for this Dissenter pure gold—unalloyed "wit and pleasure"—in the mirrors of Restoration comedy:

> In turning over the pages of the best comedies, we are almost transported to another world, and escape from this dull age to one that was all life, and whim, and mirth, and humour. . . . We are admitted behind the scenes like spectators at court, on a levee or birthday; but it is the court, the gala day of wit and pleasure, of gallantry and Charles II! What an air breathes from the name! What a rustling of silks and waving of plumes! What a sparkling of diamond ear-rings and shoe-buckles! What bright eyes, (ah, those were Waller's Sacharissa's as she passed!) what killing looks and gracefull motions! . . . Happy, thoughtless age, when kings and nobles led purely ornamental lives; when the utmost stretch of a morning's study went no farther than the choice of a sword-knot, or the adjustment of a side-curl; when the soul spoke out in all the pleasing eloquence of dress; and beaux and belles, enamoured of themselves in one another's follies, fluttered like gilded butterflies, in giddy mazes, through the walks of St. James Park.

This is from one of Hazlitt's finest bravura set-pieces, but the passage must also be characterized as an indulgence in sentiment that suppresses much unsavory truth about Restoration comedy. We are given no hint whatever here of the arrogant cruelty, not excluding even an occasional willingness to murder, that lurked in some of those "killing looks"; and we may wonder why Hazlitt, predisposed to moral censure in other literary contexts, should so willingly overlook the shameless hedonism of that "happy, thoughtless age." Indeed, it seems but a step from Hazlitt's evocation of "another world" to Lamb's view of Restoration comedy as wholly "artificial," a world of its own emancipated from moral reality—"the Utopia of gallantry, where pleasure is duty, and the manners perfect freedom." Yet there is still an important difference between Hazlitt's view and that of his friend, alike in tenor though they are. No doubt it is true that in concentrating attention on the Millamants and Fopling Flutters, both Hazlitt and Lamb were disarming the prudish conscience of their time—and perhaps their own consciences. But that Hazlitt was rationalizing away, as Sir Herbert Read contends, a "cynical realism" that Romanticism could not confront is an accusation demonstrably false, as we learn soon enough if we attend to what Hazlitt actually says of comic vision in the plays of Congreve, Wycherley, Vanbrugh, and Farquhar.

His lecture on these writers is among the more enduring chapters in Hazlitt's criticism, and it is so because he seldom loses his sense of what is historically real and what is only comically "true" in their plays. If he tries always to say the best that can be said about them, this at least is a best seldom even acknowledged as possible by critics determined to discover the worst. Nor is the best that Hazlitt sees limited to what L. C. Knights has called the "myth" of Restoration wit—the belief that brilliance of style redeems it from triviality and cynicism. That apology appears only in Hazlitt's account of Congreve, who "had by far the most wit and elegance, with less of other things." Of the dialogue in *The Way of the World*, he writes: "It is an essence almost too fine; and the sense of pleasure evaporates in an aspiration after something that seems too exquisite ever to have been realized." Hazlitt is thinking here mainly of the repartees of Millamant with her suitors; and much as he admires this heroine, he is prepared to concede that her "fine essence" is nothing if not "theatrical." For Hazlitt this quality is always the key to Congreve's style: his wit is not, nor was it meant to be, subtle perception; its "sense and satire" lie in its "artful raillery," modelled on courtly conversation, but now made more "polished and pointed" for its theatrical effect as a "new conquest over dullness." Millamant "is the ideal heroine of the comedy of high life, who arrives at the height of indifference to every thing from the height of satisfaction; to whom pleasure is as familiar as the air she draws . . . who has nothing to hope or to fear, her own caprice being the only law to herself, and rule to those about her." As such she represents the "finest idea" possible of her type, "the accomplished fine lady," translated from all its sins and blemishes in society to radiant sovereignty on the comic stage. True, Congreve "has done no more" than create one of the most artificial of artificial characters—but "if he had [attempted more], he would have done wrong."

Now this is not, as I understand it, Lamb's defense of Restoration comedy. Hazlitt's point is rather that "meretricious" manners, when comically "embellished" in a spirit that seeks only to enhance and magnify them, make their own satiric comment on themselves, even though we may come to that awareness through our delight in the extravagant frivolity or cleverness of the characters. And if not in Congreve, Hazlitt does find moral issues variously present in the other dramatists. His Wycherley, unlike Lamb's, is a writer fiercely angry at "duplicity," at least as the creator of Manly and Olivia in *The Plain Dealer*. And Farquhar implants "high principles of gallantry and honour" in the generous feelings of his otherwise "rattle-brained, thoughtless" heroes. But it is Vanbrugh who for Hazlitt most honestly—or blatantly—typifies the ambiguity of a comedy capable of moral dimension without, or with very little, moral purpose. Vanbrugh is seen as not unlike his favorite characters—"knavish, adroit adventurers," engaged in a "predatory warfare on the simplicity, follies, or vices of mankind." Yet this "cunning impudence" results in "happy and brilliant contrasts of character"—and in such "opposing" of characters Hazlitt sees the satiric dialectic at work, unconscious though it may be in serving its end. The three classes which for Hazlitt comprise nearly all the characters in Restoration comedy ("artificial elegance and courtly accomplishments" in one class, "the affectation of them" in another, and "absolute rusticity" in the third) criticize each other simply by being what they are; and out of this "conscious self-satisfaction and mutual antipathy" grows the satiric awareness, in the mind of the audience if not of the author, which finds all of them wanting as human beings.

Hazlitt's view still seems to me the most credible apology that can be offered for Restoration comedy, for it does not reduce these writers to aesthetes or entertainers, or to philosophical intellectuals, or to secret lovers of virtue. Hazlitt succeeds, I think, in demonstrating that the dramatic power (which perhaps he generally overrates) of these comedies is owing to their flirtation with the vices they "expose," and that this purely dramatic virtue had to be—and should be, under such circumstances—the primary if not the sole regard of the dramatist. The motives to satire in the theater of this age were, and could only be, motives which the satirist shared with his society: the aspiration to mannered "refinement," the most obvious sign—or test—of which is the detection and artful reproof of false pretensions. Yet to see human vanity as being mocked in these plays by a subtler variant of itself is not to acquiesce in cynicism; for Hazlitt suggests that in the very depth of the "weakness" exposed in these plays lies a transcendent source of value which survives unimpaired. As he says of a scene which reveals the "hateful" vindictiveness of Farquhar's Lady Lurewell, "The depravity would be intolerable, even in imagination, if the weakness were not ludicrous in the extreme." The saving "salt" of humor that Hazlitt finds in this comedy, its redeeming element of intersubjectivity, lies simply in the magnetism of sex, however gross, prurient, or morally ambiguous its expression. In his opening lecture Hazlitt had remarked that "there is another source of comic humour which has been but little touched on or attended to by the critics—not the infliction of casual pain, but the pursuit of uncertain pleasure and idle gallantry"; and he estimates that "half the business and gaiety of comedy turn upon" this "attraction" to "a subject that can only be glanced at indirectly . . . a sort of forbidden ground to the imagination, except under severe restrictions, which are constantly broken through." Eros, even in its most arrogant corruption, is Eros still; and Hazlitt does not hesitate to express his delight in all comic manifestations, farcically broad or delicate, of the only force of "nature" to remain unconquered by the "artificial" power of the Restoration court. Hazlitt was one son of Puritanism who did not identify, as Macaulay would, the "depravity" of the Restoration with its lust and sensuality; as we have seen, in his psychology the brutality and malice of man have their origin in the passions of the will, not in the desires of the body as such. This conviction enables Hazlitt to see in Restoration salaciousness not a fever of moral disease but a force that constantly humanizes the contempt of wit and dissolves cruelty of will into some laughable blindness or vulnerability of feeling: it is this sympathetic grace of instinct which "makes Horner decent and Millamant divine." True, in a world where "vice," that is, libertinism, was "worn as a mark of distinction," comedy was bound to degenerate at times into lustful intrigue or bawdy ribaldry; yet for all the rascality and "duplicity" that this state of affairs produces, the sense of erotic—and thus of comic—pleasure is never lost. Indeed, Hazlitt would seem to be of the opinion (though he does not expressly make the comparison) that there is more "cynical" feeling and "biting" malice toward women in Ben Jonson's comedy—in *The Silent Woman*, for instance, where the women exhibit "an utter want of principle and decency, and are equally without a sense of pleasure, taste, or elegance."

Living in an age of mounting middle-class "cant," Hazlitt recognized that neither the comic spirit nor a genuineness of moral feeling could endure if humor wholly turned its back on its original "resources" in erotic "gallantry": "Our old comedies would be invaluable, were it only for this, that they keep alive this sentiment, which still survives in all its fluttering grace and breathless palpitation on the stage." And even if the fluttering heroine should prove to be, more often than not, a wanton and a hypocrite, and if the gallant at her side should turn out to be no better than a lecherous knave, this reversal, too, is no mere jest of the Restoration but holds an everlasting lesson for moralistic critics: "One benefit of the dramatic exhibition of such characters is, that they overturn false maxims of morality, and settle accounts fairly and satisfactorily between theory and practice."

The sudden decline of Restoration comedy did not tempt Hazlitt to doubt its merit but confirmed him in his view of its excellence. The Restoration theater itself, by the very excellence of its satiric portraiture, had played no small role in furthering the process of its dissolution: "It is not the criticism which the public taste exercises upon the stage, but the criticism which the stage exercises upon public manners, that is fatal to comedy, by rendering the subject-matter of it tame, correct, and spiritless." If we look upon "the stage" here as meaning the entire theatrical tradition in its cumulative effect, as it modifies and merges with the influence of all literature upon opinion, we can still find wisdom in Hazlitt's generalization that comedy "destroys the very food on which it lives." "Comedy naturally wears itself out. . . . It holds the mirror up to nature; and men, seeing their most striking peculiarities and defects pass in gay review before them, learn either to avoid or conceal them."

The myth of decadence was perhaps even more commonly applied to comedy in Hazlitt's time than to poetry—and with good reason, for the dearth of good comedies after Sheridan was a fact that no sophisticated theatergoer would have wished to deny. Hazlitt had been proclaiming the death of modern comedy since 1813, and he was even more adamant in this prophecy than in his melancholy prognoses for painting and poetry. He dates the decline of English comedy "from the time of Farquhar," but he is too fond of that author to indict him as the first offender. Comedy had taken its fatal turn for the worse in "those *de-me-good*, lack-a-daisical, whining, make-believe comedies" of Richard Steele and others of like mind in his generation, who, bowing to the influence of Jeremy Collier and his pious denunciations, elected to write comedy "with a view not to imitate the manners but to reform the morals of the age. Some of the "good-natured malice" of the Comic Muse returned in the author of *The School for Scandal* ("perhaps the most finished and faultless comedy which we have"), but

Sheridan was the "Hesperus" of a dying tradition, and even his powers could
not consistently sustain—keep free from caricature—the truly "humorous,
or that truth of feeling which distinguishes the boundary between the absurdities of natural character and . . . gratuitous fictions." Insofar as humor,
in scattered moments, did manage to survive on the contemporary stage, it
was made subservient to farce or mixed with the "amiably mawkish"—
inspired by the wish, no longer in the least to hold manners up to ridicule,
but to flatter the attitudes of the audience. As Hazlitt wrote of one popular
specimen, Cherry's *The Soldier's Daughter*: "We are reminded of our own
boasted perfections both as men and Britons:—or if any of our follies and
weaknesses appear, they are sure to lean to the favorable side—*too much* good-
nature, *too much* gaiety and thoughtlessness, *too much* unsuspecting frankness."

Yet Hazlitt is advising no attempt to revive the old "humorous" perception. The "originals" who alone could inspire the art have vanished with
the masters who understood them; and perhaps all that might be hoped for
is that the theater honestly learn to know its bias toward sentiment for what
it is—as modern man's habitual "abstraction" from the given reality of self.
The fault did not lie merely in the fact that the characters of men in society
have been disciplined into uniformity; for moral perception itself had been
changing in that process. Men who are habitual readers no longer see each
other as individuals in some "concrete" situation of "action and circumstances," but observe each other's differences with an eye to general sentiments or, among men of reflection, to "universal truths," which are
"applicable in a degree to all things, and in their extent to none." And how
therefore could one still hope to see comic character realized distinctly and
concretely on the stage? A form essentially more abstract is needed to satisfy
modern sensibility: "We accordingly find that to genuine comedy succeed
[prose or verse] satire and novels, the one dealing in general character and
description, and the other making out particulars by the assistance of narrative and comment."

It is thus no caprice on Hazlitt's part that his lectures on the essayists
and the novelists should immediately follow that on the Restoration, or that
Steele should be praised for his attempt in the *Tatler* "to wed the graces to
the virtues" and reprobated for the same intention on the comic stage.
Hazlitt's criticism of the essayists will be deferred to the subsequent chapter,
but it is logical to deal here with his account of Swift, despite the fact that
England's greatest master of prose satire is missing from these lectures,
Hazlitt having dealt with the author of *Gulliver's Travels* in the preceding
series on the poets (where Swift also wins some rare praise for his verse).
Nothing more emphatically shows Hazlitt's instinctive resistance to the

fashion of the "amiable" than his steadfast admiration of Swift, at a time when other influential voices in criticism—Johnson, Jeffrey, Coleridge—were disparaging *Gulliver's Travels* as either too "mechanical" or too "misanthropic." Hazlitt's willingness to enjoy Swift, like his pleasure in Pope or in the Butler of *Hudibras*, is based on the recognition that literary satire is distinct from other forms of the comic, and is redeemed from its want of sympathetic pleasure by its comparative "abstraction." Many of the "disagreeable" qualities that he had castigated in Ben Jonson's comedy are welcomed as virtues in Swift, since they appear now in a form no longer grounded in a sense of individual character. Yet Hazlitt's defense of Swift's "abstraction" is not the usual line of defense for the Gloomy Dean: Swift went mad because he could not "get rid of the distinction between right and wrong," but this "constitutional preference of the true to the agreeable" was not the result of a rationalist's idealism or an ascetic's demand for moral purity but of a "literal, dry, incorrigible tenaciousness of . . . understanding" which gave him "his soreness and impatience of the least absurdity." Hence the "playful" element in Swift is his "sensible" irony about the deceptive appearances of "sense," and his only fancifulness—or all that his genius needed—was "the sparkling effervescence of his gall" as he withdrew from reality to devise a consistent counter-world of his own, one that would expose "the prejudices of sense." And in this enterprise Hazlitt discerns, without adverting to the culture of the period, the secret affinity of Swift's satire with modern science: "He has tried an experiment upon human life, and sifted its pretensions from the alloy of circumstances; he has measured it with a rule, has weighed it in a balance, and found it, for the most part, wanting and worthless—in substance and in shew." Was the result, then, "misanthropy?" "What presumption," Hazlitt sardonically answers, "and what *malice prepense*, to shew men what they are, and to teach them what they ought to be!" Hazlitt might well have paused to explain just how that last teaching survives so pessimistic a demonstration as Book Four of the *Travels*; but at least his reading of Swift anticipates most scholarly consensus today that the satire of the *Travels* was designed, not to ridicule man's suppressed animality, his want of reason or conscience as such, but "to shew the insignificance or the grossness of our overweening self-love"—of man's "empty pride." "It is," Hazlitt concludes, "an attempt to tear off the mask of imposture from the world; and nothing but imposture has a right to complain of it."

Hazlitt had always insisted that "the proper object of ridicule is *egotism*," whether worldly or intellectual; and to note this constant theme in his praise of satire—and in his own satire, we might add—is to be made aware again of the political motive in his willingness to see traditional comedy die. Why lament the passing from the theater of genuinely dramatic characters, with their laughable bagwigs and swords, if the same historical process has "driven our fops and bullies off the stage of common life?" There might remain "the same fund of absurdity and prejudice in the world as ever," but the very force of self-love in mankind, now made sensitive to the novel "power" of such ridicule as Swift's or Voltaire's, would insure that the selfishness of "arbitrary" power could never again seduce human consciousness into sanctioning, or accepting without question, the systematic or prescriptive violation of the rights of self-love in others. In this thought we may discern why Hazlitt prizes satire and "comedy of manners" over "comedy of nature"; and indeed we begin to understand now that Hazlitt sees essentially the same continuity of moral tendency in all phases and modes of comedy. The process by which individual humors had passed in the Restoration into uniform "pretensions" of class superiority was also a process of "enlargement" mediated by a "generalization" of taste whose counterpart is the modern "diffusion" of knowledge. And the growth of sentimental comedy and prose satire was symptomatic of a more advanced phase of the same expansion of consciousness into a force of "public opinion" which transcends class lines and transforms "manners" into norms of conduct no longer based on "dress" and modes of speech but on "private sentiment and public morals," that is, intersubjective values. However uncreative, or averse to genius, all this "abstraction" might be, it accords with "the natural progress of things . . . with the ceaseless tendency of the human mind from the *Finite* to the *Infinite*."

Hazlitt would now, however, always take so benign a view of the human comedy's triumph over itself. A greater evil than "egotism" might be breeding in the world, a peculiarly modern evil of inwardly "levelling" uniformity whose consequences for the quality of life and thought might be far worse than the mere "want of character" in modern imagination. Something of this fear is heard—although, being mixed with Hazlitt's inherited myth of history, there is still no suggestion, as there will be in the twenties, that the "levelling" tendency is virulent and destructive of civilization—in this brilliant hail-and-farewell to the comedy of "character":

> It is, indeed, the evident tendency of all literature to generalise
> and *dissipate* character, by giving men the same artificial education
> . . . so that . . . all men become alike mere readers—spectators,
> not actors in the scene, and lose all proper personal identity. The
> templar, the wit, the man of pleasure, and the man of fashion,
> the courtier and the citizen, the knight and the squire, the lover

and the miser—[and here follows a long list of names of famous specimens of these and other types in comic literature] . . . have all met, and exchanged common-places on the barren plains of the *haute littérature*—toil slowly on to the Temple of Science, seen a long way off upon a level, and end in one dull compound of politics, criticism, chemistry, and metaphysics!

This was written in 1813, and although the prophecy was repeated in the last of the lectures on comedy, it is by no means Hazlitt's last word on the future of "character" in modern literature. For this was conceived before the advent of Scott's novels, and Hazlitt was to learn from the regeneration of the novel in his time to discover some unexpected and redeeming benefits for literary imagination in the continued ascendancy of science and other forms of modern "abstraction".

In his lecture "On the English Novelists" (much of which repeats a long review-essay written for the *Edinburgh* in 1815), Hazlitt is still content to describe his critical effort, in this relatively unfrequented "department of criticism," as one "toward settling the standard of excellence, both as to degree and kind, in these several writers"—writers still assumed to be, however philosophical, "comic writers," engaged like their fellows in the humorous or satiric depiction of "manners," though in "the airy medium of romance." Clearly Hazlitt in these words is still accepting the traditional identity of the novel as an impure form of comedy or romance—or, in Johnson's description, as "the comedy of romance"—and only in incidental observations does the lecturer begin to move toward that original conception of the novel, emerging in fragments and by slow degrees over the next ten years, for which Hazlitt has never been given sufficient credit. And how original for its time that conception was may be inferred from a remark of his three years hence: "Good novels are . . . the most authentic as well as most accessible repositories of the natural history and philosophy of the species." The novelist had often been called a "historian," but it was breaking new ground to suggest that the modern writer of fiction might also be a kind of scientist, a philosophical experimenter refining upon his observations in the laboratory of fictional invention. Here was a comparison which is no longer, as in Hazlitt's praise of Swift, a mere analogy; here it points the way toward the modern independence of the novel from other forms, as a genre with its own laws of character development and its own methods of representing "truth."

Hazlitt had learned from Fielding to begin an account of the novel with Cervantes. Although Hazlitt places *Don Quixote* in the category of "comedy of nature," Cervantes is praised as "the inventor of a new style of writing," for "there is no work which combines so much whimsical invention with such an air of truth." "The whole work breathes that air of romance, that aspiration after imaginary good, that indescribable longing after something more than we possess, that in all places and in all conditions of life,

'—still prompts the eternal sigh,
For which we wish to live, or dare to die!' "

And Hazlitt then proceeds to contrast this spirit of "romance" with the more purely comic genius of Fielding, who does not draw "lofty characters or strong passions," and whose nearest approach to a "romantic" character is Parson Adams in *Joseph Andrews*. Hazlitt remarks that the Don and Sancho "do not so much belong to, as form a class by themselves," and being no less "original" than "ideal," they "identify themselves more readily with our imagination," with the result that "the blows and wounds" incurred by this pair in their grotesque adventures haunt the memory and have exercised throughout Europe a "healing influence" on "many a hurt mind." But after hinting at this unprecedented intimacy of relationship between fictional character and the self of the reader, Hazlitt obscures his insight by resorting to the language of his comic theory. He describes "truth" in *Don Quixote* as perfect "keeping in comic character," or "consistency in absurdity"—essentially the same in principle as truth of "the ludicrous" in stage comedy, the principal difference being, presumably, that humor in Cervantes invariably relates to imaginative aspiration.

Clearer signs of Hazlitt's feeling for the distinctive powers of the novel begin to emerge when Fielding is compared with Smollett. The humor in Smollett, Hazlitt observes, "arises from the situation of the persons, or the peculiarity of their external appearance," almost never, as in Fielding, from some surprising but inevitable fitness of the incidents to the characters of the persons involved. Smollett "exhibits the ridiculous accidents and reverses to which human life is liable," but Fielding reveals "the stuff of which it is composed." Fielding's "subtlety of observation on the springs of human conduct . . . is only equalled by the ingenuity of contrivance in bringing those springs into play, in such a manner as to lay open their smallest irregularity." Again Hazlitt draws the parallel with modern science: "The detection is always complete, and made with the certainty of skill of a philosophical experiment, and the obviousness and familiarity of a casual observation." Fielding's excellence is thus neither great wit nor humor but "profound knowledge of human nature," and especially of "what may be called the *double entendre* of character," surprising us—as in the case of the "demure" but "equivocal" Mrs. Bennet in *Amelia*—"no less by what he leaves in the dark (hardly known to the persons themselves) than by . . . [his] unexpected discoveries."

Hazlitt in these perceptions is on the verge of breaking through to the distinctive psychological potential of the novel, but the comic-satiric tradition of "truth" is still too strong in his mind. He speaks of the "vast variety" of life in *Tom Jones*, but the phrase barely hints at the epic quality of that novel; and Hazlitt, determined to regard his author as using "incident and situation only to bring out character," fails to discern the purely novelistic relationship between Fielding's hero and the novel's panoramic vision of English society. Hazlitt was never quite happy with Tom as a hero: he confessed to "a lurking suspicion that Jones was but an awkward fellow," a slave to "headlong impulse," and perhaps not very admirable except for "a morality of good-nature which in him is made a foil to principle." What Hazlitt fails to see is that the conflict between principle and natural impulse, between the morally heroic and the unheroic, is the true dialectic of the novel that Cervantes and Fielding had discovered: the progress toward discovery of this truth of experience by the hero—or by the reader, but most often by both—constitutes the true "development" of the story. For unlike the hero of pure romance, who embodies an ideal of virtue that society already admires, the hero of the novel is made to undertake his journey through society in order to learn the difference between ideal and fact, between inward virtue or truth and its outward simulation—or (to use Lionel Trilling's terms) between reality and appearance. The relative weakness of this dialectic in the eighteenth-century novel helps to explain Hazlitt's uncertain grasp of it; and we should note that his dissatisfaction with these novelists points to precisely this weakness. He had spoken of the power of imagination in Cervantes as an "involuntary unity of purpose"; and his objection to all the eighteenth-century novelists is that their "energy of purpose" is either, as in Fielding, too slight or, as in Richardson, too conscious of its ends. When he praises Richardson for "intense activity of mind" and a power of "reasoning imagination" capable of linking character to "ideal forms," he comes close to recognizing in these qualities a significant advance beyond Fielding's essentially theatrical conception of the novel. *Pamela*, for instance, is described, but only in passing, as the educational biography of a self: "The interest of the story increases with the dawn of understanding and reflection in the heroine." Hazlitt is distracted from pursuing this insight by the lesser problem of Richardson's epistolary method, whose excessive rationalism lures our critic into the mistake of judging Richardson by the standards of Fielding's realism. No doubt it is true that Richardson fallaciously endows his characters with "the presence of mind of the author," but, as Hazlitt himself concedes, the entire and complex "chain" of motive, event, and consequence—the "wonderful chain of interest"—is brilliantly revealed by this artifice, so that "everything is brought home in its full force to the mind of the reader also." Hazlitt looks no farther into the paradox of this "artificial reality"; and his remarks trail off in wonder at the "peculiarity" of a writer who could create such miracles of moral interest as Clarissa and Lovelace yet "systematically prefer" to both so monstrous a moral coxcomb as Sir Charles Grandison.

Hazlitt's comments on the author of *Tristram Shandy* are brief and slight, but he does capture the essential paradox in Sterne: "a vein of dry, sarcastic humour, and of extreme tenderness of feeling," which merge in a wit that is "poignant, though artificial." What chiefly interests Hazlitt in the non-heroic, "hobby-horse" whimsy of Sterne is its cultural aspect, its expression of its time. Hazlitt asks himself now why "our four best novel-writers" should have appeared in the same period with Hogarth, the first periodical essayists, domestic tragedy and "the middle style" in stage comedy. Waiving more general causes, he gives a political explanation: after 1688 and the Hanoverian Succession, "it was found high time that the people should be represented in books as well as in Parliament." Hazlitt's own politics tend to color this account, but essentially he sees, and is the first critic to see, the new direction in literature as a middle-class phenomenon: "In despotic countries, human nature is not of sufficient importance. . . . The *canaille* are objects of disgust rather than curiosity; and there are no middle classes." Uncle Toby and his creator could now appear in the world of English fiction because, under a dispensation that secured "person and property," the English individual "had a certain ground-plot of his own to cultivate his particular humours in." This insight into the shaping of literary forms (not merely of their intellectual content) by the cultural milieu represents one of the birth moments of a genuinely historical criticism: Hazlitt here, as Tave remarks, "seizes the central fact," though we must note that the change in sensibility is dated somewhat too late. And when he turns to the novels of his own time, Hazlitt's historical sense is even more apparent, although its articulation is more troubled and ambivalent. He is aware that such new departures as Gothic fiction had challenged "the ancient *regime* of novel-writing" but how deep that innovative challenge was, or could become, he himself was slow to learn, as his judgments here on Scott suggest.

This first report on the Waverley Novels is favorable but scarcely enthusiastic. Hazlitt deplores the absence in the "author of Waverley" (not yet identified as Scott) of the Cervantesque "ideal" quality ("the author has all power given him from without—he has not, perhaps, an equal power from within"), and he misses, too, the mediating sympathy of a Fielding, perhaps even the conscience of a Richardson: "In the midst of all this phantasmagoria, the author himself never appears to take part with his characters, to prompt our affection to the good, or sharpen our antipathy to the bad." Behind this complaint there lurks, too, a prejudicial aversion that Hazlitt had felt to Shakespeare's history plays ("Something whispers us that we have no right to . . . turn the truth of things into the puppet and plaything of our fancies," and this prejudice had led Hazlitt in 1816 to declare outright: "We do not like novels founded on facts." It is, in short, "imagination and passion" that he looks for in Scott and fails to find in any intense degree: he fails, that is, to see and appreciate the mode of their presence, although he is probably right about the limited degree of their power. Yet five years later, in *The Spirit of the Age*, Hazlitt very differently balances the same account. What had hitherto been reckoned a deficiency in endowment now becomes the distinguishing mark of Scott's genius and its wealth of resources: a generic weakness has bred an original and compensatory strength. Novelistic imagination is here no longer conceived as bound to the "ideal" imagination of romance; indeed, Scott's genius is seen now as a power justly rebelling against the dominion of standards borrowed from poetry: "Sir Walter has found out (oh, rare discovery) that facts are better than fiction; that there is no romance like the romance of real life; and that if we can but arrive at what men feel, do, and say in striking and singular situations, the result will be 'more lively, audible, and full of vent,' than the fine-spun cobwebs of the brain." Scott is still described as "only the amanuensis of truth and history," but now Hazlitt adds: "It is impossible to say how fine his writings in consequence are, unless we could describe how fine nature is." But it is the commentary on Scott's characters that chiefly registers Hazlitt's change in attitude. He had said in his lecture that the characters of this novelist "appear like tapestry figures . . . the obvious patchwork of tradition and history," but now we are told that by this method Scott "has enriched his own genius with everlasting variety, truth, and freedom." And as proof Hazlitt offers a stunning pageant, two pages in length, of more than forty Scott characters, which he summons individually from his memory, citing for each some quality or act or association which makes them unforgettable. this new catalogue has the air of a Homeric roll-call; it is a conscious tribute to the epic range of Scott's knowledge of humanity. "What a host of associations!" Hazlitt exclaims in his peroration; "What a thing is human life! What a power is that of genius! What a world of thought and feeling is thus rescued from oblivion!"

In this sense of a novelistic "world," of a perspective on "human life"
distinct from or transcending the individual life, Hazlitt was at last re-
sponding to the dimension of "truth" peculiar to the novel, or at least to
the nineteenth-century novel. What we have in this praise is essentially a
vision of the novel as the Balzacian *comédie humaine*—a "comedy" as different
from comedy in the old sense as from romance, for this is the creation of a
"world" which no longer depends for its interest on a poignant blend of
pathos and humor rooted in individual character, or on some preconceived
judgment of the congruity or rationality of human behavior. It is significant
that Hazlitt no longer taxes Scott with moral indifference to his characters;
that indifference, indeed, is now seen as inseparable from Scott's unique
merit as a novelist—"the candour of Sir Walter's historic pen." Scott "treats
of the strength or the infirmity of the human mind, of the virtue or vices
of the human breast, as they are to be found blended in the whole race of
mankind." Hazlitt never dwelt long enough on this insight to note its
implicit challenge to eighteenth-century precedents, or to relate it to his
own myth of history as progressive "abstraction"; but if he had, he might
have seen how the novel was escaping from the dilemma posed by the modern
atrophy of the sense of concrete individuality. What modern "abstraction"
had really been producing, in Scott as in his greatest contemporary critic,
was a historical sense of society and a cultural sense of personality. Mindful
always of Scott's Toryism and his Caledonian pride, Hazlitt preferred to see
only the pastness, the primitivism, the nostalgia in Scott's created world;
and this is why he continues to speak of the historical element in the novels,
not as their very center, but as the "background," again by implied analogy
with a painter's canvas. And Hazlitt continues also to call attention to the
weakness of the dramatic foreground, even though Scott "is the most dramatic writer now living." Hazlitt vigorously protested the contemporary
habit of likening the Great Unknown to Shakespeare; and he noted that
Scott's heroes, all too reminiscent of the "insipid" heroes of popular romance,
"do not act, but are acted upon." That, no doubt, is Scott's limitation, but
it was surely also his originality to represent for the first time the individual
will as being acted upon, in the very depths of the mind and heart, by
historical forces. And there was, too, another kind of force operative in Scott
which linked in an original way the historical changes of the past to the
timeless world of romance—and, by indirect reaction in the reader's imagination, to the modern world. If we wonder what, in terms of Hazlitt's own
psychology of the self, the new dimension of inward power was that so
forcibly struck him in his reading of Scott sometime after 1819, we shall
find it, I think, in this passage from "On the Pleasure of Hating" (1823):

The secret of the *Scotch Novels* is . . . [that] they carry us back
to the feuds, the heart-burnings, the havoc, the dismay, the
wrongs and the revenge of a barbarous age and people—to the
rooted prejudices and deadly animosities of sects and parties in
politics and religion, and of contending chiefs and clans in war
and intrigue. We feel the full force of the spirit of hatred with
all of them in turn. As we read, we throw aside the trammels
of civilization, the flimsy veil of humanity. "Off, you lendings!"
The wild beast resumes its sway within us, we feel like hunting-
animals, and as the hound starts in his sleep and rushes on the
chase in fancy, the heart rouses itself in its native lair, and utters
a wild cry of joy, at being restored once more to freedom and
lawless, unrestrained impulses.

No one could wish for a clearer recognition in Hazlitt's time of the
role of the repressed unconscious self in shaping modern literary imagination,
It should go without saying how far this vision of modern delight in fiction
differs from Hazlitt's earlier picture of the bemused reader of Sterne—the
middle-class Hanoverian Whig, congratulating himself on his escape from
Popery and content to cultivate the garden of his amiable humors. Hazlitt
has here put firmly behind him the aura of benevolist sentimentality that
occasionally hangs over his aesthetic principle of "sympathy"; here his dissatisfaction with Fielding's ethic of "good-nature" finds potent articulation.
And perhaps the growth of Hazlitt's admiration of Scott's novels may be
most simply explained as the realization that, even in their tendency to
glorify the loyalties of the barbarous past, their author was serving the cause
of sympathetic imagination more purely than any of his liberal and nobly
self-conscious contemporaries. What for Hazlitt redeems the fascination with
"lawless" violence in Scott is not only the enlargement of the sense of
"humanity" but its constant accompaniment, on the conscious level, with
manifestly empirical fact: the love of power is here not indulged in Gothic
fantasy but made to enforce the sense of inescapable reality. Only indisputably
known and sharply realized facts, or those things of lore and legend which
wield the power of fact in popular memory—something whose existence is
still relevant to national or to historical consciousness, yet securely removed
from the conscious temperings of modern will—could enable that will truly
to go out of itself, whether in reader or writer. "Fiction," Hazlitt cautions
in a late review (1829), "to be good for anything, must not be in the author's
mind, but belong to the age or country in which he lives."
        Charles I. Patterson, who judges Hazlitt's criticism of the novel to be

"the first clear and well-defined conception of fiction from a great English critic," has aptly interpreted his doctrine for the novel to mean that "the actual condition is the conceptual" in the author's imagination. But I would add to this formulation the corollary that for Hazlitt the conceptual in fiction ought to function, or functions best, as a conception *of* the actual—or, more precisely, of the factual, of some recorded or observed "circumstance" which is or once was real (or believed to have been real) in the world of events, and which provides the novelist with an incontestable substance, a "material" basis, for his inventive experiment. There is a brief essay of 1829 which corroborates this point: the essay stands as Hazlitt's last known comment on Scott, and in it the impact of the Waverley Novels at last takes the form of some theoretic generalizations about novelistic imagination. Hazlitt was answering an objection made to Scott's recent habit of appending to his novels historical and other notes, which a writer in the *London* had deplored as an ugly unveiling of "machinery" that must spoil the imaginative effect. The question, Hazlitt saw, involves the entire problem of the relation of the novelists's art to life:

> Fiction is not necessarily the mere production of fancy, although much fancy is to be found in works of fiction; nor is it essential that fiction should be untrue. . . . It is not a stage illusion, nor a magic lantern, presenting shadows and spectacles that either burlesque or flatter humanity; but a transcript from nature, in which the truth is preserved not *literally*, but *poetically*. . . . The plain fact will not constitute a novel; there must be the creative spirit to work up all its parts into an embellished picture, and superadd such matters as, although not actually true, are deducible from that which is, and are relatively consistent. . . . The question then is, how far our pleasure will be interrupted by the assurance that certain portions are real, and how far our confidence in the rest will be thereby shaken. To know that [in *The Heart of Midlothian*, which Hazlitt thought Scott's finest novel] Effie Deans lived and was accused is not likely to produce a disbelief in the remaining parts of her story, *which if not literally true might have been so, and seem as if they could not be dispensed with without violating the congruity of the whole* [my italics]. Her history is not the less touching because historical evidence does not attest it scene by scene; while its appeal to our feelings is enhanced by our knowledge that the main incident did happen, from which all the other details and circumstances appear to spring naturally.

. . . To be vexed at the shock our first enthusiasm might receive [from the notes] would be weakness or vanity; we should have known that there was a secret process going forward; if we did not know it, it is our vanity that is hurt at the exposure. . . . A true relish for nature can neither be deceived by a bad fiction, nor dissipated by the most prosaic illustrations.

With this formulation of the novel's distinctive "truth," no longer to be confused with that of romance or comic theater, Hazlitt may be said to have provided aesthetic warrant for new creative possibilities that would soon appear in nineteenth-century fiction to belie his prophecy of the necessary inanition of modern literature. Hazlitt has here fully adapted to conditions of imagination in the novel his aesthetic of intersubjective sympathy: we should note that sympathy not only with the leading characters but with the "creative spirit" of the novelist makes the "secret process" go forward: we not only are but *should* be aware of the authorial presence just as—to cite an analogy that Hazlitt draws in the same essay—we are and should be aware of the puppet-master's strings and of the wood and paint of his figures, for it is that awareness which makes their actions seem both pleasurable and real to imagination. This, then, is Hazlitt's modification of the parallel with a scientific experiment: the "process" differs from its cultural model in being one in which the observer participates. The novel, in short, is neither more nor less objective than any other form of art; its function is not to reveal a truth in a world conceived as existing entirely beyond art but an aspect of truth implicit in all the arts; its "poetic" process differs from poetry in being not merely the symbolic intensification of value, but the symbolic articulation of historical and other "plain fact" in its significance for value.

Obviously there are delicate problems in relating realistic to symbolic "truth" in the novel that Hazlitt's theory ignores; he would have been a very clairvoyant critic, indeed, if he had detected and isolated such problems so early in the century. Like so much of his speculation, his vision of the novel is left undeveloped in its own right, but less, I suspect, because of habitual imprecision than because of the pressure of other issues that could not be denied their claims upon his waning time and energies in his final decade. The transition we have been observing in his theory of fiction from perspectives of "nature" and "ideal" imagination to perspectives of "real life," of history and necessities of "the age," was not something precipitated, as perhaps I have so far suggested, by the impact of Scott's genius; rather, his growing sense of Scott's importance expresses the deepening aggravation

of the passional conflict in himself—a conflict that had been growing steadily
more complex and demanding, both in its inward stresses and in its effects
upon his career and his life in society. The transition in theory becomes one,
therefore, in its motivating logic, with the transformation, after 1819, of
the public lecturer into the personal essayist—into a writer performing his
own experiment on "human life," in order to understand and save, once and
for all, his living gifts of power from neglect or attrition by an increasingly
hostile world, as well as from the estranging piety of a myth of moral "truth"
that had hitherto dominated his sense of identity.

MICHAEL FOOT

The Shakespeare Prose Writer

Happy are they who live in the dream of their own existence, and see all things in the light of their own minds; who walk by faith and hope; to whom the guiding star of their youth still shines from afar, and into whom the spirit of the world has not entered! They have not been "hurt by the archers," nor has the iron entered their souls. The world has no hand on them.
From Hazlitt's essay *Mind and Motive*, and occasionally repeated by him elsewhere.

William Hazlitt, in all his glory, at the peak of his powers, still faced a furiously hostile world. Since he would not budge an inch in his opinions, he might have become irredeemably embittered or broken altogether. Instead, he transmuted the way in which he defended his principles into a new serenity.

Born on 10 April 1778, it was not until he was twenty years old, in the year 1798 ("the figures that compose that date are to me like 'the dreaded name of Demogorgon' ") that his individual spirit was truly awakened, and not until twenty-five years later again that he described that experience in *"My First Acquaintance with Poets"*, the greatest essay in the English language.

A year or so later he produced his best book of collected essays, *The Spirit of the Age*. Therein he pinioned, mocked, revalued or extolled some two dozen of his most famous contemporaries with an insight and wit which none of his would-be imitators have ever been able to capture. One after another he chipped away at the pedestals of popular heroes, or bestowed upon them a fresh glow of understanding, often anticipating with precision the verdicts of posterity. He was no respecter of conventional judgements

From *Debts of Honour*. © 1980 by Michael Foot. Davis-Poynter Limited, 1980.

from left, right or centre—crusted Tories might find themselves "nearly" forgiven; so-called reformers were rebuked when they befuddled themselves with too much of the milk of human kindness; and those who usually came off worst of all were the whiffling moderates in the middle, "ever strong upon the stronger side," like *The Times* newspaper (yes, even in those days). He hated the inhumanities which his fellow-citizens inflicted upon one another in the world around him; yet he loved the other worlds in which he and they lived, the world of nature, of books, of the theatre, of painting, of music; indeed the whole wide world of the imagination in which he had seen "the prospect of human happiness and glory ascending like the steps of Jacob's ladder in a bright and never-ending succession." All these assorted moods and aspirations and freshly-shaped nuances of judgement he poured into *The Spirit of the Age* with a newly-confident profusion.

And yet this masterpiece of a lifetime was abruptly dismissed as too pert and extravagant by the best-known, most genial, Whiggish editor of the day, Francis Jeffrey, and it is impossible to believe that Hazlitt's scorn of the Whigs was not the true cause of a disapprobation so misplaced. (Editors have never been quite the same breed since, for Hazlitt retaliated with an essay which should keep them in their place for eternity—"They are dreadfully afraid there should be anything behind the Editor's chair greater than the Editor's chair. That is a scandal to be prevented at all risk.") Yet even before Jeffrey had rushed to the defence of his Whig dinner-friends, a printer with a fair enough record for courage thought it judicious at first to publish the volume anonymously, and the suspicion persists that either he or the author or the two together did not wish to risk immediate association on publication day with another volume which had appeared two years before, also published anonymously, but at once unmasked as something too indescribably foul to be mentioned in decent society: Hazlitt's *Liber Amoris*, the product, it was supposed, then and now, of a mind diseased, not to mention a lascivious body and soul.

But let us, for a half-moment at least, leave Hazlitt, the self-confessed fool of love, to return to his unforgettable first acquaintance with poets. Smitten though he still was by the attentions or non-attentions of Sarah Walker, and enfolded in that essay as his customary laments for her cold embraces undoubtedly were ("my heart has never found, nor will it ever find, a heart to speak to"), yet he can recall, with an exhilaration which still tingles in every sentence, all his richest memories, his youth, his father, the first books he read, the first meeting with Coleridge, the visit to Llangollen, "the cradle of a new existence," the journey to Nether Stowey, the first hearing of the *Lyrical Ballads* from the lips of Wordsworth himself (all in that self-same sacred year of 1798), "and the sense of a new spirit in poetry came over me."

No man ever treasured his youth more joyously than Hazlitt did; no man ever honoured his father better; no man ever discharged with such good faith the debts of honour he owed to the favourite authors of his youth— Burke, Rousseau, Cervantes, Montaigne and a legion more. No critic (except perhaps a few fellow poets, and not many of them) ever heard the strange language of a new school of poetry with such an alert sympathy, and certainly no critic ever welcomed the innovation with greater daring and, despite all subsequent political feuds, with more persistence and warmth.

All these claims can be sustained from the evidence offered in this single essay, written when the love-diseased Hazlitt was, on his own testimony, still in a most desperate condition—"I have wanted only one thing to make me happy, but wanting that, have wanted everything!" There he is again, in the very same essay, bewailing Sarah in one sentence and still in the next quite capable of inflicting one of his most well-considered swipes at Coleridge, and one to be upheld by the scrutiny of modern scholars. It was Hazlitt who first put his finger, without the substantial proof provided since, on Coleridge's addictive plagiarism.

Yet the attempt to rest so heavy a weight on a single essay leaves one wrong impression. It might be truer to say the opposite, as Hazlitt himself said of Burke: that the only specimen of his writing is *all that he wrote*. In literature, Hazlitt relished the old and welcomed the new. He saw how (and was one of the very first to remark how) Shakespeare achieved "the combination of the greatest extremes." He himself liked to see all sides of a subject, never for the purpose of searching out some muddled middle ground but rather to force an explosive fusion or an entirely new departure. One of his friends bound Burke's *Reflections on the French Revolution* and Thomas Paine's *Rights of Man* between the same covers and said that together they made a good book. A similar treatment could be applied to Hazlitt's writings. Many of his essays seem to be written in pairs, each presenting opposite aspects of the case, one, maybe, suffused with the romantic spirit unloosed by Rousseau and the other relentlessly reasserting Hazlitt's conviction that men must not only talk and dream, but act. Always he would still strive to extract the effective conclusion from the clash of contrasts. No such dreamer was ever less of a dilettante. No critic was ever more of a self-critic.

Any such claim would have provoked squeals of protest from those apostate politicians or apostate poets whom Hazlitt berated so fiercely in his lifetime. But most of them never had the chance of reading his *Conversations of Northcote*, which was published in full only after his death. Many good reasons for reading the *Conversations* may be offered—their sheer readability, the individual charm of the old Plymouth painter, the wonderful assortment of irrelevancies and curiosities which both Northcote and Hazlitt contributed to the pile. But it is hard to escape the belief that Hazlitt had a deeper, if unconscious, purpose. He somehow put into Northcote's mouth most of the current criticisms or condemnations of himself, and then struggled, not always successfully, to find the right retort.

This, unconsciously also perhaps, was what Hazlitt set out to achieve on a much more spacious canvas. Ever since he had carried home in triumph from Shrewsbury to Wem his first book by Edmund Burke, he had been dazzled by that style which he revered more than any other—"His words are the most like things; his style is the most strictly suited to the subject." Hazlitt's own style owed more to Burke's than to anybody's, but he was never primarily a student of style despite his many apposite remarks upon it. The thing mattered more than the word. Literature was not something removed from life; the two were endlessly intertwined. Books were weapons in the cause of human freedom.

How, then, could Hazlitt, the great rebel, respect Burke, the great apostate? Burke had "stood at the prow of the vessel of state, and with his glittering, pointed spear *harpooned* the Leviathan of the French Revolution." How could Hazlitt, the arch-champion of the French Revolution, pay such honour to him? It was not merely the magnanimous gesture of one writer to another across the gulf of politics. The kinship between the two men went much deeper. Hazlitt saw the truth and force of so much that Burke was saying; no man could write like that and tell lies. Burke's understanding of mankind, he said, was "inexhaustible as the human heart, and various as the sources of nature." Yet this mighty intellect had somehow been used to persuade the people of England that "Liberty was an illiberal, hollow sound; that humanity was a barbarous modern invention; that prejudices were the test of truth, that reason was a strumpet and right a fiction." To explain the phenomenon, the mechanism of politics must be taken to pieces. And somehow Burke must be answered. "He presents to you," Hazlitt wrote, "one view of the face of society. Let him who thinks he can, give the reverse side with equal force, beauty and clearness . . ." Hazlitt's life work was his great reply. He gave to the English Left a perspective and philosophy as widely ranging as Burke had given to the English Right.

Hazlitt was not content with the multitude of swift retorts provoked by Burke's *Reflections on the French Revolution*. He was one of the first to recognise that the formidable pamphleteer Thomas Paine, author of *Rights of Man*, the most famous and enduring of all the replies, was a great writer.

But neither Paine nor William Godwin, nor the poets with their dreams of Utopia, less still the men of the calibre of Sir James Mackintosh, could prevail against Burke, and not all their defeats were due to the power wielded by authority. The first rebuffs made many of them abandon their creed and go over to the enemy. A toughter fibre was needed, a creed of human freedom more firmly founded on the rock. No one was ever more excited by the soaring hopes unloosed by the French Revolution than Hazlitt; he soaked himself in the romantic prophets; Rousseau's *Confessions* and *La Nouvelle Héloïse* made him shed tears. He accepted to the full the reformers' doctrine that "men do not become what by nature they are meant to be, but what society makes them." And society could be transformed; the French Revolution looked like romance in action. But the deed would not be done by utopians who would never soil their hands, nor by an arid appeal to reason alone, nor by the economists and utilitarians who inherited the tattered mantle of the revolutionaries.

Thus, Hazlitt was a romantic in revolt against extreme romanticism; he loved the ardour of it and hated the egotism. He was an idealist who knew that present enemies must be fought here and now, tooth and nail, on their own ground; a passionate believer in man's benevolence and his perfectibility, but one who recognised as well as Burke that passion and prejudice could not easily be uprooted from the human heart. Since the passions could be good and the right traditions should be revered, why should they be? They too could be enlisted in the Good Cause. The core of his theory had been worked out in the first *Essay on the Principles of Human Action*. It was vastly illustrated in all his later writings. He tried to separate the wheat from the chaff in the bountiful harvest of new ideas which were sprouting up all around him. He searched for a synthesis between Rousseau and Burke. And they dared call him a bigot!

His politics left their brand on every aspect of his writing, just as they governed or disrupted his personal relationships. Someone said that he took his politics around with him, like a giant mastiff, and love me, love my dog was his motto. (Only Sarah was allowed a special dispensation; it is not recorded that he lectured *her* on the evils of legitimacy, although he did present her with a treasured statuette of Napoleon.) But the tide of his political ideas flooded into every cove and inlet of his thought. 1798 was not only the year of the *Lyrical Ballads*; it was also the year of the Reverend Doctor Malthus's *Essay on the Principle of Population as it affects the Future Improvement of Society*. How soon Hazlitt became acquainted and obsessed with this curious literary phenomenon is not clear, but he was certainly the first reader to appreciate to the full the menacing nature of the apparition.

Here, it is true, society was offered a philosophy for the rich, an economic textbook for Tories, a faith as firm as a mathematical equation which could salve their conscience and cast the cloak of religion over the whole scene of human wretchedness in the England of his time. "Malthus," wrote Hazlitt, "had given to the principle of population a personal existence, conceiving of it as a sort of infant Hercules, as one of that terrific giant brood, which you can only master by strangling it in its cradle." And that in turn was how Hazlitt set about Malthus. Without the advantage or encumbrance of expert economic knowledge, with irony and logic and passionate indignation, he exposed the moral consequences of Malthus's infamous clerical decrees.

He thereby anticipated not merely the reply of the economists decades later but the whole temper of nineteenth-century radicalism. He brushed aside the patronising charity of those who would "take nothing from the rich and give it to the poor," and defended the right to strike with the fervour of a Chartist or a twentieth-century syndicalist. His essays on prison reform and on Benthamism raced beyond the plodding precepts of the utilitarians and came nearer to the ideas of modern psychology. "Men act from passions, and we can only judge of passions by sympathy." Criminals, like the world itself, could not be changed by preaching. Somehow the institutions of society must be changed, and men must show the will to do it. There Hazlitt did not differ much from his fellow-reformers, but he added his own ingredient to the reforming creed of his time. The reformers themselves needed to understand the human heart if they were to get men to move, and if they were not themselves, in the face of setbacks, to abandon or betray their cause. So many of the reformers of his time—Robert Owen, for example—who talked so much about the rights of men, knew so little about the passions of men. A whole curriculum of schooling for reformers could be compiled from the writings of Hazlitt whom the nervous nineteenth century would have preferred to dismiss as a wayward romantic essayist. In his mind the interaction between words and deeds could never be severed. And the next immediate deed in the struggle, *the one that mattered*, was never long absent form his reckoning. Perhaps the most remarkable of all Hazlitt's feats in imaginative sympathy was the way he, the supreme no-compromiser, nonetheless understood the exigencies of practical politicians.

He wrote about political ideas and political history, about the immediate controversies of the age, about the motives of politicians, about political parties and the conduct within parties, about the resolute capacity of those who hold power and the chronic failings of the reformers and revolutionaries who would seek to wrest it from them. His themes were as perennial as Burke's. Of course his own heroes both in history and in his own time were the iconoclasts, the intransigents, the rebels who would not bend with the storm or droop in the sunshine; their example suited his own situation and soothed his pride. But his understanding of the art of politics was not limited by the experience of his own defeats. "Ambition is in some sort genius," he said. Here is his picture of what a statesman could be. It is rarely quoted: but has it ever been bettered?

> To use means to ends, to set causes in motion, to wield the machine of society, to subject the wills of others to your own, to manage abler men than yourself by means of that which is stronger in them than their wisdom, viz, their weakness and their folly, to calculate the resistance of ignorance and prejudice to your designs, and by obviating to turn them to account, to foresee a long, obscure and complicated train of events, of chances and openings of success, to unwind the web of others' policy, and weave your own out of it, to judge the effects of things not in the abstract but with reference to all their bearings, ramifications and impediments, to understand character thoroughly, to see latent talent and lurking treachery, to know mankind for what they are, and use them as they deserve, to have a purpose steadily in view and to effect it after removing every obstacle, to master others and to be true to yourself, asks power and knowledge, both nerves and brain.

A naïve extremist, unaware of the realities of politics, could not have written that sentence.

It was not only that he could appreciate the politicians of the past—say, Cromwell, with "his fine, frank, rough, pimply face and wily policy" (Hazlitt was accused of having a pimply face, which doubtless encouraged the show of sympathy); he looked down from the gallery of the House of Commons on the performers below, and had his own list of preferences which can scarcely have accorded with anyone else's, especially those on the left. He preferred Castlereagh to Canning ("One of those spontaneous mechanical sallies of his resembles a *voluntary* played on a barrel organ"), Burdett to Brougham ("He is not a backbone debater. He wants nerve, he wants impetuosity"), the real would-be doers to the self-conscious rhetoricians with all their finical flexibility of purpose and character.

Hazlitt exerted a comparable independence of judgement in every other field too. Naturally he liked to discern the virtues of those whose political views he shared. Not only was he the first to recognise Thomas Paine's literary qualities; he saw also, and won more jeers from fashionable critics for recognising that William Cobbett's "plain, broad, down-right English" made him "one of the best writers in the language." Of course he paid special honour to the great radical writers of the past, John Milton, Andrew Marvell and many more. But he also wrote more enthusiastically than any previous English critic on a host of others who at first sight might be imagined to have no political hold on him at all—Swift, Pope, Montaigne, Fielding, Cervantes: above all, Shakespeare. Others, like Coleridge, alongside Hazlitt (not anyone hardly *before* him), were encompassing Shakespeare in a new glory. But it was Hazlitt's criticisms which had immediate and lasting impact on two of his greatest contemporaries in Europe, Heinrich Heine and Henri Beyle, alias Stendhal, both of whom came to London and carried the new Shakespearian fashions back across the Channel.

Both Heine and Stendhal acknowledged the debt they owed to Hazlitt, which is more than can be said for Wordsworth or Coleridge. Despite his deepening political quarrels with them, Hazlitt never ceased to honour Wordsworth as the great originating poet of the age, and Coleridge still held the central place in his essay as the man who had opened his understanding, "till the light of his genius shone into my soul, like the sun's rays glittering in the puddles of the road."

But intertwined with the tributes—inextricably, as Hazlitt doubtless intended to make sure—were the searing, indelible invectives against those who had deserted the cause of their youth. Wordsworth and Coleridge may be forgiven if they failed to turn their Christian cheeks; what they should never be forgiven—for neither were exactly paragons of sexual virtue—were the Lakeside libels against Hazlitt's alleged sexual antics which they unloosed, not in any sudden fit of outrage at the time, but long after the unspecified exploits had supposedly occurred. However, the point concerns not the Wordsworth-cum-Coleridge intolerance, but Hazlitt's magnanimity. Long after he had plentiful evidence of the venomous gossip with which they had pursued him, even to the point of threatening his most treasured friendships with the Lambs and Leigh Hunt, he still would not be shifted from his recognition of their greatness. Literary cliques are not noted for their generosity. Hazlitt refused to be suffocated even when he had been driven, by the pressures of politics, into a clique of one.

However, for all his readiness to stand alone, for all his gift for solitude, his individuality won him some unexpected or idiosyncratic friends—John Cavanagh, the fives player, or William Bewick, the engraver, or James Northcote, the portrait painter, or William Hone, the allegedly blasphemous bookseller, or the young ex-medical student who came to his lectures, accompanied him on the journeys to Leigh Hunt in the Vale of Health on

Hampstead Heath, and who had shown "the greatest promise of genius of any poet of his day." Hazlitt, alas, never wrote a full-scale essay on John Keats, but almost every fresh study reinforces Keats's own testimony of how intricate and all-pervasive was the Hazlitt influence upon him. "The whole cadence of his (Keats's) prose," writes Robert Gittings, "is that of Hazlitt whose reviews he seems to have had nearly by heart." It was Hazlitt lecturing at the Institution across Blackfriars Bridge, or Hazlitt talking on the walk to Hampstead, or Hazlitt writing in Leigh Hunt's *Examiner*, who was responsible for most of the introductions which made Keats a poet—to Shakespeare, to Wordsworth and several more. In particular, it was Hazlitt who introduced Keats to his favourite Wordsworthian poem, *The Excursion*, at a time when Wordsworth was still rejected and neglected in fashionable quarters. Here was just another example of Hazlitt's "disinterestedness" which Keats so much admired and emulated. Keats, of course, shared Hazlitt's political aversions, as he discovered to his disquiet when he called at Wordsworth's home in the Lakes only to find that the poet of cloud and cataract was out canvassing for the Cumberland Tories. Anyhow, thanks to modern scholarship and Mr. Gittings more especially, the truth is now established beyond challenge. Henceforth Keats and Hazlitt climb Parnassus roped together, and a terrible curse of combined Hazlittean/Keatsian power must fall upon anyone who would tear them apart.

What other critic in English literary history, or any other literary history for that matter, ever had such a pupil? And yet poetry was not Hazlitt's first love, and never even at any time his all-consuming passion. He had set out in early youth to become a painter, and he made good use of all he learnt, becoming (in the words of Lord Clark) "the best English critic before Ruskin." He was there at the Drury Lane theatre on the night of Edmund Kean's first appearance as Shylock, and the meeting was one of the most memorable in the history of the English theatre. He was, as Professor R. L. Brett has written, "the first critic to take the novel seriously." Yet none of these pursuits were the ones which touched him most closely. His pride was that he was a philosopher. In that first essay describing his meeting with the poets he tells of the tears he wept in the long, and at first vain, exertion to get words on to paper. It was nearly six years after the sacred year of 1798 before he finally succeeded in completing his little-read and not-easily-readable *Essay on the Principles of Human Action*. Like other painfully delivered first children, it remained his favourite, especially as no one else showed any liking for the brat.

He finished that first book at the age of twenty-six; he died at the age of fifty-two. What he truly wrote in that bare quarter-of-a-century interval was a vast, rambling, astringent, Montaigne-like autobiography, which abjured all the self-worshipping postures both he and Keats so much detested, but which yet succeeds in telling as much as any man ever told about his convictions, his tastes, his emotions, his enthusiasms, and how he strove perpetually to subject them to the most severe tests at his command. It is surely this open invitation to explore the well-nigh inexhaustible resources, "the whole compass and circuit of his mind," which makes the titles "essayist" or "critic" such feeble terms to describe what he sought to accomplish.

Some fine biographers have already made the exploration too, notably P. P. Howe, the devoted and inspired editor of his *Collected Works*, or Herschel Baker, author of the only volume which deserves to be set alongside Howe's, and, on a lower shelf, Hesketh Pearson's *The Fool of Love*, and Augustine Birrell's not-to-be-despised pre-1914 volume. For a real addition to the existing store of knowledge we shall have to await the forthcoming new biography by the wisest as well as the most thorough of Hazlitt scholars, Professor Stanley Jones, whose contributions to the learned journals have already disposed of several anti-Hazlitt canards.

Meantime, let us return afresh to Hazlitt's evidence against himself. Very few themes which figured prominently in his life are left in an unfinished state in his writings. One concerns his religion, and it is indeed surprising that one born and bred as a Celtic dissenter, one who shared so eagerly the Puritan vision of his country's history, one who knew every step in John Bunyan's pilgrimage, one who would have fought and died for the true religion's cause at Burford, one who indeed wrote about every other subject under the sun, hardly ever made any direct reference to any religious topic, less still any religious conviction. He mocked the Papists, ("Nothing to be said against their religion but that it is contrary to reason and common sense"), side-kicked the Presbyterians ("Weighing their doubts and scruples to the division of a hair, and shivering on the narrow brink that divides philosophy from religion"), damned the Methodists ("They plunge without remorse into hell's flames, soar on the wings of divine love, are carried away with the motions of the spirit, are lost in the abyss of unfathomable mysteries—election, reprobation, predestination—and revel in a sea of boundless nonsense"), heaped secular scorn on the Laodicean Anglicans ("Satan lies in wait for them in a pinch of snuff, in a plate of buttered toast, in the kidney end of a loin of veal"), and extolled the true Dissenters for keeping their covenant, as the stars keep their courses. But he avoided all deep religious arguments, and one reason may be that he wished to give no open offence to his father. He himself had been intended for the Unitarian Ministry and he knew how his family were disappointed when he was seduced from that vocation by his first dream that one day he would be able to say with Correggio: "I also am a painter," and, even more, by his later resolve to pursue the wicked trade of Swift, Defoe and such-like infidels. But the tact of father and son, towards each other if towards no one else, was such that no shadow was allowed to fall across their relationship. What would have happened if Sarah Walker had appeared on the scene while his father was still alive, none can tell.

Suddenly, when Sarah did make her first appearance, or rather when "with a waving air she goes along the corridor," his life was transformed and he became "the very fool of Love." It is the only corner of his love life which Hazlitt has revealed, and the evidence has naturally been pursued by scholars with prurient dedication. He himself wrote a classic "confession"; however, it is his reticence which may first deserve consideration.

Considering how original were Hazlitt's ideas on almost every theme which captivated him, considering how he could race ahead to anticipate the thought, in the field of psychology, say, no less than politics, of the whole ensuing century, it is the more surprising that he never seemed to turn his mind to the great question of the rights of women. He was certainly no feminist, not that the word had yet been invented nor even that the thing itself was common. He was a frequent visitor at the house of William Godwin, and one of his gleaming sentences casts a kindly ray of light across the countenance of Mary Wollstonecraft. Yet the extraordinary fact is that he did not write much more about her; seemingly, he had never read her *Vindication of the Rights of Woman* or it left no mark whatever.

For Hazlitt, as for most of his contemporaries of a similar cast of mind, the great romantic bible was Rousseau's *La Nouvelle Héloïse*, which was still also a revolutionary document. Enough for the moment, enough for one century perhaps, to break the love-making conventions of polite, ruling-class society. Hazlitt's ideal of womanhood, I suspect, was Rossini's Rosina whose liberation took the form of enabling her to twist men round her little finger, without them having the foggiest notion what she was up to, and no bad choice either; who in his senses ever could resist her? However, in real life, for Hazlitt, Rosina was transformed into Sarah Walker, and she almost destroyed him with her wiles, her titillations, her prevarications and her treacheries. (Let it not be forgotten, by the way, that no one has ever told Sarah's side of the story: what a find that would be!) Yet despite the absence of the slightest touch of feminism in his makeup, Hazlitt was not a male chauvinist; more like a male pacifist indeed, and his debasement before the idol of his own creation came near to encompassing his ruin then and thereafter.

He could not keep quiet on the subject, stopping to tell everybody about his bewitchment in every tavern from Chancery Lane to Covent Garden. He unloosed a gushing flood upon her fawn-like head and upon his few especial long-suffering friends. Then he turned aside from most other labours to compile and publish anonymously the *New Pygmalion*, the *Liber Amoris*. One of his letters to Sarah—and perhaps even the most presentable—fell into the scurrilous hands of a Tory journal, *John Bull*, and was reproduced, with much sneering and snivelling, to damn him and his politics to eternity. Some of his eminent ex-friends—like Coleridge, for example—to their immortal dishonour, used the occasion to resuscitate an old unproved and unprovable charge that the young Hazlitt had been the villain in some terrible seduction scene (some have even called it "rape," without a tincture of evidence) twenty years before. He was soon having to publish anonymously also his *Spirit of the Age* essays—some of the greatest in the English language—for fear of inviting too swift an association with "the impotent sensualist," the lascivious author of *Liber Amoris*.

Fashions, of course, have changed altogether about the *Liber Amoris*. Robert Louis Stevenson was so shocked by it that he gave up the idea of writing Hazlitt's life. Augustine Birrell, whose biography was otherwise intelligently sympathetic, wished to consign the offending volume to "the realms of things unspeakable, fit only for the midden." Even the most learned and authoritative of modern biographers, Herschel Baker, turns aside in horror from Hazlitt in love, and even Professor R. L. Brett, a most eminent Coleridgean, invokes the *Liber Amoris* to justify some of the old libels on Hazlitt's youthful sex-life. How Coleridge and Wordsworth would have rubbed their pious hands at the thought. And yet in modern times too Hazlitt has been better enabled to speak for himself. In the excellent Penguin *Selected Writings* (published in 1970 and edited by Ronald Blythe), the *Liber Amoris* is printed in full but also printed where it ought to be, alongside his other writings, and Ronald Blythe also gives proper recognition to two others before him who have helped rescue the book from the midden.

It was indeed only as late as 1948—well over a hundred years after that "sweet apparition," or, if you wish, that "slimy, marble varnished fiend" had turned her glance so fatally upon him—that any commentator appreciated to the full the nature of Hazlitt's agony. Charles Morgan wrote in that year an entirely new kind of introduction to the despised volume in which he invoked the case-knowledge of modern psychology, partly to explain Hazlitt but, even more remarkably, to reveal how much of modern discoveries in this field Hazlitt had anticipated. Morgan also made a most discriminating comparison between Hazlitt and Stendhal, Hazlitt's contemporary whom he resembled in so many aspects, although most notably *not* in philandering bravado or technique. Just at the moment when Hazlitt was making obeisance before the statue he had erected, Stendhal was writing his own book of love, *De l'Amour*, in which the Hazlittean trauma, disease, madness, idyll, is immortally diagnosed.

Soon afterwards the two men met in Paris. Stendhal gave his book to Hazlitt who must have read it on his journey onwards towards the two mistresses they shared, Rome and Venice. I have often wondered: how Hazlitt's hair must have stood on end as he turned over those burning pages; how he must have marvelled at this French sympathiser who understood his predicament with Sarah so much better than his own countrymen; (and how he must have concealed the volume from his new sedate wife who was making part of the journey with him). "She is dead to me, but what she once was to me can never die." That was Hazlitt's own epitaph on the affair, but perhaps Stendhal and Montaigne even helped finally to soothe his passion. And as Morgan shows, there was one sense in which he carried the investigation further even than these two acknowledged mentors; he "shows"— in the words of Morgan—"because he is a supreme realist and is unafraid to give himself away, that the crystallising lover is by no means the blind fool that he is traditionally supposed to be. He thus deprives himself of the only romantic defence with which an aloof and self-righteous world might be disposed contemptuously to cover him. The lover, Hazlitt says in effect, is not even a dupe; he is worse, he is a half-dupe, and yet persists." Hazlitt made himself, again in Morgan's memorable conclusion, "the sane, unsparing analyst of his own madness." And yet Stendhal conducted the analysis afresh, and with an even greater clinical precision, and with a sense of humour too (and even with an invocation of the name of Montaigne, sacred to Hazlitt certainly), to recall sexual fiascos as remarkable as his own. Hazlitt surely must have been gratified to be assured, after such painful torture and on such high combined authority, that he was not so abnormal a creture after all.

As for Hazlitt's sanity, so often and interestedly questioned by his political enemies, his friends may take pleasure from the fact that plumb in the middle of the months when he obsessively and vainly waited for a soft word from Sarah, he could still sit down and write a five thousand word letter to his ten-year-old son (suitable for later publication, to be sure), one of the most civilised documents ever written by any father to any son:

It is a good rule to hope for the best . . . Never anticipate evils
. . . Learn never to conceive prejudice against others, because

> you know nothing of them . . . Never despise anyone for anything
> he cannot help—least of all for his poverty . . . Never despise
> anyone at all . . . True equality is the only true morality or true
> wisdom . . . Believe all the good you can of everyone . . . Envy
> none, and you need envy no one . . . Never quarrel with tried
> friends or those whom you wish to continue such . . . Be neither
> a martyr, nor sycophant . . . Do not gratify the enemies of liberty
> by putting yourself at their mercy . . .

So the sentences and the elaborations tumble onto the page one after another; no one could doubt the coolness and the reflective wisdom which he had achieved by sheer intellectual exertion, and yet in the midst of it he is well nigh overthrown by the tempestuous nature of his passion. And, a month or two later again, he had governed his temper afresh, and the so-called besotted bigot had returned to his favourite addiction of seeking to explain the other side of the question.

Certainly no condemnation was intended when Hazlitt, the romantic realist, insisted:

> Women have often more of what is called good sense than men.
> They have fewer pretensions; are less implicated in theories; and
> judge of objects more from their immediate and involuntary
> impression on the mind, and therefore more truly and naturally.
> They cannot reason wrong; for they do not reason at all. They
> do not think or speak by rule; and they have in general more
> eloquence and wit, as well as sense, on that account. By their
> wit, sense and eloquence together, they generally contrive to
> govern their husbands.

The compliment was barbed, but it was a compliment no less.

With or without the help of psycho-analytical treatment from "my friend Mr. Beyle," Hazlitt did recover. The period of six or seven years, between his escape from Sarah's listless clutches and his death in 1830, is not by any reckoning a famous one in English history, and for Hazlitt especially it must have seemed craven and squalid. All his soaring political hopes had been shattered; Jacob's ladder had collapsed. No proper acclaim for his literary powers came from most of his fellow-countrymen; he was still an outcast. He embarked on what even his few remaining devoted friends considered to be a chronic wastage of his talents, a monumental *Life of Napoleon*, which threatened to bury him altogether. Money troubles hit him harder even than ever before; for the first time in his life he spent some months in prison for debt. Yet neither his courage nor his genius were impaired. On the contrary: made ridiculous in love, staring political defeat in the face, libelled by his enemies, harried by creditors, the Hazlitt who was often upbraided for ill-temper wrote with an ever-increasing equilibrium, almost optimism. He reasserted the convictions of his youth with something of the old exhilaration, and not only in the field of politics, and he did it with mellowness but without a hint of retreat, without a jot of weakness or cynicism.

> Really it is wonderful how little the worse I am for fifteen years
> wear and tear, how I came upon my legs again on the ground of
> truth and nature, and "look abroad into universality," forgetting
> there is any such person as myself in the world.

How little diseased was that mind. T. S. Eliot wrote of Matthew Arnold that "he had no real serenity, only an impeccable demeanour." Hazlitt's demeanour could outrage everybody, even the long-suffering Charles Lamb. But, contrary to the impression left by his unfailing pugnacity, he had achieved a real serenity—as the later essays, one after another, prove. It was not that he had become complacent or withdrawn from the battle. He was still in the thick of it, giving blow for blow, whenever the opportunity occurred. But the poets, who in the words of his friend Keats "pour out a balm upon the world," gave a specially healing dose to Hazlitt. He had fought a good fight; he had kept the faith. "One source of this unbendingness (which some may call obstinacy)," he wrote in "*A Farewell to Essay Writing*,"

> is that, though living much alone, I have never worshipped the
> Echo, I see plainly enough that black is not white, that the grass
> is green, that kings are not their subjects; and in such self-evident
> cases do not think it necessary to collate my opinions with the
> received prejudices.

None could stop him thinking for himself; he was secure in that citadel and could survey the battlefield from its turrets. And he knew too (and who will dare deny the claim?) that "in seeking for truth I sometimes found beauty." Above all, he stayed young, "kept the candid brow and elastic spring of youth." The iron had not entered his soul although too many folk then and since thought it was uniquely constructed of nothing else.

He is, wrote William Bewick, "the Shakespeare prose writer of our glorious century; he outdoes all in truth, style and originality." That was the view expressed by the excited young art student who attended one of Hazlitt's lectures in the company of the equally excited John Keats. Very

few agreed with them at the time, and when he died, the political furies
which had beaten upon him while he lived did not quickly abate. However,
through the influence of his own writings, his literary reputation has steadily
increased until now, two hundred odd years after his birth, it stands higher
than it ever did. William Bewick's tribute no longer looks like a youthful
exaggeration.

JOHN L. MAHONEY

Imagination and the Ways of Genius

We see the thing ourselves, and shew it to others as we feel it to exist, and as, in spite of ourselves, we are compelled to think of it. The imagination, by thus embodying and turning them to shape, gives an obvious relief to the indistinct and importunate cravings of the will.—We do not wish the thing to be so; but we wish it to appear such as it is. For knowledge is conscious power; and the mind is no longer, in this case, the dupe, though it may be the victim of vice or folly.

—"On Poetry in General"

Paralleling Hazlitt's concern with disinterestedness and sympathy as central values for the artist and the work of art is his elevation of the imagination as the power through which these values are achieved. One should stress the description of it as a power, since Hazlitt, like so many of his contemporary critics, was given to discussing imagination, not as a mere picture-making faculty or a compartment of the mind, but as a larger and more comprehensive capability which synthesized and unified the many resources of the human mind.

Hazlitt's debt to eighteenth-century British empiricism has, of course, been stressed. The scorn of abstraction, the emphasis on the primacy of experience in any theory of knowledge, the powers of association and coalescence—these are lifelong tenets of his critical credo. Yet, as he grew older, he rejected or modified the more mechanistic dimensions of the empirical tradition. Indeed, what is distinctive about Hazlitt is not only his peculiar approach to and modification of empirical theory, his use of experience as a

From *The Logic of Passion: The Literary Criticism of William Hazlitt*. © 1978 by John L. Mahoney. Fordham University Press, 1981.

foundation stone, but his addition of new and quite dramatic ideas on the mind's ability to mold and develop experience in accordance with its own desires and images. In Professor Albrecht's words, he "retains the mind's dependence on the senses but stresses its ability to deal creatively with the materials of sensation. As Hazlitt describes it, the mind can mold these materials into ideas and symbols, to which, through sympathetic identification, it gives objective truth and moral urgency." Hazlitt, as he proceeded, revealed increasingly the impact of eighteenth-century Anglo-Scottish aesthetic theory. No longer is imagination regarded as a kind of variation of memory to be trusted only when its products are firmly anchored in a narrowly conceived reality. No longer is its value to be seen only in terms of its control by the judgment. One senses in Hazlitt's critical writing a liberation of imagination, an emphasis on its freedom to create and on its distinctive modes of operation, a consistent stress on its significance as a basis of moral conduct. He made the sharpest kind of distinction between reason and imagination. Reason, the remote, cold, and analytic power, is simply inadequate as a basis for moral or analytic judgment, and its inadequacy can be seen in three specific descriptions which he offers: "1. Abstract truth, as distinct from local impressions or individual partialities; 2. Calm, inflexible self-will, as distinct from passion; 3. Dry matter of fact or reality, as distinct from sentimentality or poetry." Imagination, the immediate, warm, and synthetic power, is triggered by strong feeling; "the warmth of passion is sure to kindle the light of imagination on the objects around it."

Imagination, then, is above all else a creative power, with that rare ability to shape its materials into a new reality which heightens our sense of the reality we see and hear. Strong passion triggers the imagination to seek and struggle for a mode of embodying the sometimes wild and indistinct cravings of the mind and will. The basic concern of imagination is, not with things as they are, but rather with things as they are touched by the peculiar electricity of our psychic lives. At times only the imagination, with its wondrous powers, can begin to match the infinitely varied responses evoked by the power of human passion; only the imagination can reveal a thing as it is felt to exist and as a human is compelled to think of it. In a quite brilliant passage, Hazlitt dramatizes the process as it relates to the imagination of the artist:

> Let an object be presented to the senses in a state of agitation and fear—and the imagination will magnify the object, and convert it into whatever is most proper to encourage the fear. It is the same in all other cases in which poetry speaks the language

of the imagination. The language is not the less true to nature because it is false in point of fact; but so much the more true and natural, if it conveys the impression which the object under the influence of passion makes on the mind. We compare a man of gigantic stature to a tower; not that he is any thing like so large, but because the excess of his size, beyond what we are accustomed to expect, produces a greater feeling of magnitude and ponderous strength than an object of ten times the same dimensions. Things, in short, are equal in the imagination, which have the power of affecting the mind with an equal degree of terror, admiration, delight, or love. When Lear calls upon the Heavens to avenge his cause, "for they are old like him," there is nothing extravagant or impious in this sublime identification of his age with theirs; for there is no other image which could do justice to the agonising sense of his wrongs and his despair!

To the objection to Milton's *Lycidas* on the grounds that it combined Christian religion with the fictions of a heathen mythology, Hazlitt replied strongly that although such a juxtaposition may seem grotesque to the limited power of the reason or understanding, to the imagination it is completely proper. Indeed, every classical scholar, even the most orthodox Christian, is at heart an honest heathen; the characters of pagan mythology have a reality beyond mere names, and it is this reality, with all its beauty and sublimity, which captures the imagination of Milton and other poets. Edmund Burke generally gave secondary attention to facts; "they were the playthings of his mind." To the man of great imagination "things that are probable are elevated into the rank of realities. To those who can reason on the essences of things, or who can invent according to nature, the experimental proof is of little value. This was the case with Burke." *Don Quixote* offers something "more stately, more romantic, and at the same time more real to the imagination than any other hero upon record." Apart from *Robinson Crusoe*, Defoe's fiction is too tied to fact and a narrow norm of realism which cramps the creativity of the imagination. Richardson's fiction, in spite of its artificial world, outdoes that of Fielding and Smollett in imagination. Although Fielding is a wonderfully natural observer of a great variety of human character, and Smollett a great caricaturist of eccentricity, Richardson is the imaginative novelist *par excellence*, creating, as he does in *Pamela*, a reality nowhere else to be met.

Among his contemporaries Wordsworth is a strong exemplar of the creative imagination who creates his own materials and whose poem *The*

Excursion "paints the outgoings of his own heart, the shapings of his own fancy." Dividing poetry into two major classes, that of imagination and that of sentiment, Hazlitt described the poetry of imagination as "calling up images of the most pleasing or striking kind" and the poetry of sentiment as depending on the "strength of the interest which it excites in given objects." The greatest poetry combines the best of both kinds of imagination, and Chaucer, Spenser, Shakespeare, and Milton exemplify them in the highest degree. Young and Cowley, dazzled by the ingenuity and exuberance of their own invention, lack quality of emotion. Wordsworth, possessed of extraordinary feeling, is

> deficient in fanciful invention: his writings exhibit all the internal power, without the external form of poetry. . . . Either from the predominant habit of his mind, not requiring the stimulus of outward impressions, or from the want of an imagination teeming with various forms, he takes the common everyday events and objects of Nature, or rather seeks those that are the most simple and barren of effect; but he adds to them a weight of interest from the resources of his own mind, which makes the most insignificant things serious and even formidable.

Walter Scott lacked this creative impulse, what Hazlitt called "this plastic power, this capacity of reacting on his first impressions." Whereas the true poet is "essentially a *maker*," Scott was a "learned, a literal, a *matter-of-fact* expounder of truth or fable." He was fundamentally an artist of the external whose strength was in large part in the richness of his materials, unlike Shakespeare whose great gift was in moving beyond the given materials to give them new life, new form, new meaning through the great creative powers of his imagination.

Imagination, then, is truly creative and has that rare ability to shape its materials into a new reality with a life and justification of its own. Again sounding like so many Anglo-Scottish theorists on the imagination's powers of coalescence and association and yet bringing to his own speculations a new vitality, he speaks of the imagination as an "exaggerating and exclusive faculty" above the demands of the logical and literal. In the interests of providing the sharpest focus and the greatest possible effect for an object of range and significance, it borrows from one thing to heighten another, it accumulates details and circumstances into a new unity. One is reminded of Keats's memorable phrase that the excellence of every art lies in its intensity by which all disagreeables evaporate, with essentials heightened and accidentals minimized. Reason or understanding, on the contrary, divides and measures, judging of things not in terms of their immediate effect on the mind, but according to their connections with one another. Whereas the imagination is basically a monopolizing power, willing to violate superficial ideals of equality and proportion in the interests of passionate intensity and realization, reason is distributive, weighing the relative merits of things in accordance with some abstract standard of ultimate good.

In its operations the imagination constantly associates, and its association transcends any merely mechanical process through a much more subjective association of objects and impressions. In defining the law of association, "as laid down by physiologists," as a process in which "any impression in a series can recal any other impression in that series without going through the whole in order: so that the mind drops the intermediate links, and passes on rapidly and by stealth to the more striking effects of pleasure or pain which have naturally taken the strongest hold of it," he reveals his roots in the eighteenth-century associationist tradition extending from Hobbes to Hartley. In his much less mechanical and much more poetical analysis of the source for "our love of Nature as for all our habitual attachments" as the principle of association, he reveals his wariness about the limitations of empirical psychology and his own special need to bring the elements of human sensitivity and freedom to bear on a peculiar source of aesthetic pleasure. The setting sun, he argues, moves him deeply not so much from the beauty of the phenomenon itself as from its power to recall numberless thoughts and feelings which over the years have touched him deeply. "I remember," he recalls, "when I was abroad, the trees, and grass, and wet leaves, rustling in the walks of the Thuilleries, seemed to be as much English, to be as much the same trees and grass, that I had always been used to, as the sun shining over my head was the same sun which I saw in England." Yet he notes a difference when it comes to human beings. In the Tuileries

> the faces only were foreign to me. Whence comes this difference? It arises from our always imperceptibly connecting the idea of the individual with man, and only the idea of the class with natural objects. . . . The springs that move the human form, and make it friendly or adverse to me, lie hid within it. There is an infinity of motives, passions, and ideas, contained in that narrow compass, of which I know nothing, and in which I have no share.

Imagination, which Hazlitt described as an intuitive perception of the hidden analogy of things, has an uncanny ability to penetrate to the core of a reality, to separate the essential from the nonessential, to determine when a thing is related intimately to a system or is only an exception to it. The "excesses committed by the victorious besiegers of a town," he reasoned, "do not attach to the nation committing them, but to the nature of that sort of warfare, and are common to both sides. They may be struck off the score of national prejudices. The cruelties exercised upon slaves, on the other hand, grow out of the relations between master and slave; and the mind intuitively revolts at them as such." Shakespeare's associative powers are enormous; his imagination is plastic and its movement rapid and circuitous. His images combine remoteness with telling familiarity; indeed, unlike many Metaphysical conceits, their fundamental truth to nature and closeness to human concerns seem a result of the ways in which unlike points of comparisons are yoked into a new kinship. Spenser, the poet of romance in *The Faerie Queene*, can evoke the mood of distant terror or imaginary distress; his descriptions, especially those of the Cave of Despair, the Cave of Mammon, or the change of Malbecco into Jealousy, assume "a character of vastness and sublimity seen through the same visionary medium, and blended with the appalling associations of preternatural agency." Chaucer's special beauty lies in his intense concentration on and revelation of the essential in his characters of *The Canterbury Tales*. Although he touches on the many facets of personality in his creations, the overall impression is sharp and to the point. "The chain of his story is composed of a number of fine links, closely connected together, and rivetted by a single blow."

The imagination's greatest power, however, is sympathy, its ability to project, to enter into another reality, and to share its being. Again revealing a debt to eighteenth-century moral theorists, Hazlitt nevertheless goes beyond them in stressing the imagination's activity. Unlike memory and sensation, which are directed to the past and present, the imagination is future-oriented and free from the intimidations of past and present. Even the child, in pulling his hand from the fire or moving his lips to quench his thirst, reveals the futuristic or anticipatory thrust of the imagination "by means of which alone I can anticipate future objects, or be interested in them" and which can "carry me out of myself into the feelings of others by one and the same process by which I am thrown forward as it were into my future being, and interested in it."

Hazlitt's practical criticism abounds in examples of the sympathetic and anticipatory imagination at work, but few are more suggestive than his treatment of *Romeo and Juliet*. His more general remarks about the play reveal, of course, a good deal of the enthusiastic response and the spirit of evocation which characterize his admiration of Shakespearean drama. "Nature," he says in describing his response to the play, "seems to put forth all its freshness; and the heart throbs with its full weight of joy, too soon changed to woe. The golden cup of pleasure, mantling to the brim, is dashed with bitterness: the intoxicating draught of youth, of hope, of love, drowning and ravishing the sense, is suddenly turned to poison." There is, however, as is so often the case in Hazlitt's approach to literature, a more systematic and analytic attempt to understand the special pleasure conveyed by the drama and its characters, and this attempt is very much rooted in Hazlitt's conception of the futuristic and anticipatory powers of the imagination. Shakespeare, he contends, cannot be understood in terms in Renaissance or indeed of eighteenth-century ideas of the role of imagination. As Hazlitt puts it, "Shakespear has but followed nature, which existed in his time, as well as now. The modern philosophy, which reduces the whole theory of the mind to habitual impressions, and leaves the natural impulses of passion and imagination out of the account, had not then been discovered; or if it had, would have been little calculated for the uses of poetry." Such a philosophy, and its inability to explain the intensity and magic of our earliest experiences, occasioned Wordsworth's Platonic answer to the problem of the *Immortality Ode*, an answer which Hazlitt deems unsatisfactory. "It is not from the knowledge of the past that first impressions of things derive their gloss and splendour, but from our ignorance of the future, which fills the void to come with the warmth of our desires, with our gayest hopes, and brightest fancies." It is this ignorance of the future and the anticipation which accompanies it which is so true to the nature of things and goes such a long way toward an understanding of the emotional states of Romeo and Juliet. Theirs are lives, not of reminiscence, but of vital anticipation kindled by the deeply sympathetic qualities of the imagination. Shakespeare, in Hazlitt's conception,

> has founded the passion of the two lovers not on the pleasures they had experienced, but on all the pleasures they had *not* experienced. All that was to come of life was theirs. At that untried source of promised happiness they slaked their thirst, and the first eager draught made them drunk with love and joy. . . . Desire has no limit but itself. Passion, the love and expectation of pleasure, is infinite, extravagant, inexhaustible, till experience comes to check and kill it.

Romeo and Hamlet, although very different characters in many ways, are alike in the character of their imaginations. "Both are absent and self-involved, both live out of themselves in a world of imagination. Hamlet is abstracted from every thing; Romeo is abstracted from every thing but his love, and lost in it."

It is this conviction that "Desire and imagination are inmates of the human breast," that the sympathetic quality and futuristic orientation of the human imagination can be a source of great moral and aesthetic beauty, which serves as the fundamental premiss of Hazlitt's perceptive and memorable observations on *Romeo and Juliet*. Countless other Shakespearean examples can be cited. There is, of course, the memorable comment on the two major characters in *Antony and Cleopatra*, especially on the extraordinary sensitivity revealed in a single statement of Cleopatra's. Recalling her musings on Antony's thoughts and actions during their absence, Hazlitt remembers her " 'He's speaking now, or murmuring, where's my serpent of old Nile?' " and says: "How fine to make Cleopatra have this consciousness of her own character, and to make her feel that it is this for which Antony is in love with her!" The greatness of the line he attributes to an "intuitive power, the same faculty of bringing every object in nature, whether present or absent, before the mind's eye."

The intensity of passion in *King Lear*, the speed of action and wildness of imagination in *Macbeth*, and the rapid shifts of feeling in *Othello*, all of which Hazlitt attributed to the breadth of Shakespearean sympathy, are exceeded only by the brilliance and perfect dramatic truth of *Hamlet*. Its hero is marked not so much by passion or will as by refinement of thought and feeling; the play forces no interest, leaving everything "to time and circumstances." The "events succeed each other as matters of course, the characters think, and speak and act just as they would do, if they were left to themselves." Such is the character of Shakespeare's imagination in these plays and in the creation of these characters. "His characters are real beings of flesh and blood; they speak like men, not like authors. One might suppose that he had stood by at the time, and had overheard what passed."

Hotspur's rage when Henry IV forbids him to speak of Mortimer and his lack of sensitivity to all that his father and uncle do to assuage his feelings is a marvelous cameo to Hazlitt. It is, he says, as if Shakespeare made his imagination the handmaid of nature. "He appears to have been all the characters, and in all the situations he describes. It is as if either he had had all their feelings, or had lent them all his genius to express themselves." *Measure for Measure*, on the contrary, is less effective as a play because "there is in general a want of passion; the affections are at a stand; our sympathies are repulsed and defeated in all directions." *The Tempest* he regarded as one of Shakespeare's most original and perfect plays and the characters of Caliban and Ariel as examples of the magic of their creator's imagination. Caliban is an almost miraculous creation, "the essence of grossness, but there is not a particle of vulgarity in it"; the character's brutal mind is portrayed in contact with the original and pure forms of nature. "It seems almost to have been dug out of the ground, with a soul instinctively superadded to it answering to its wants and origin."

Hogarth's figures, Fielding's major characters, the Elizabethan dramatists—these and so many other examples underline Hazlitt's preoccupation with the imagination in its sympathetic dimension and his praise for it as a major root of the imagination's ability to create beauty which is truth and truth which is beauty. So often in reading Keats's letters, especially those in which he singles out Shakespeare for special praise because of his selflessness and impersonality, one hears sharp echoes of the great critic whose lectures Keats attended and whose critical posture he admired so much.

Imagination is the key manifestation of genius, another subject of great significance in Hazlitt's aesthetics and practical criticism. Indeed, in some ways the terms are practically synonymous. Such an attitude, of course, represents an almost complete change from the speculation which characterized much Neoclassic theory, and the change parallels in striking fashion the general shifting of critical priorities between 1660 and 1800. Hazlitt's speculations on the idea of genius were occasioned, to a great extent, by the rather familiar Neoclassic dichotomy between original genius and imitation, the chief spokesman of which was Sir Joshua Reynolds. Many Neoclassic critics, Dryden, Pope, and Johnson in particular, believed that it was not originality, but the acceptance and guidance of past models which produced the true work, and Pope's "Learn hence for ancient rules a just esteem / To copy Nature is to copy them" became a kind of motto. Reynolds, whose *Discourses* are an admirably representative example of eighteenth-century critical principles, had written quite decisively that "by imitation only, variety and even originality of invention is produced. I will go further! even genius, at least what is generally called so, is the child of imitation" because "genius cannot subsist on its own stock."

Hazlitt in his essay "On Genius and Originality" opposed Reynolds' basic assumptions, arguing that any notion of connecting genius with accumulation of knowledge is seriously defective. For him it is "a power of original observation and invention," and "a work demonstrates genius exactly as it contains what is to be found no where else, or in proportion to what we add to the ideas of others from our own stores, and not to what we receive from them." It is, "for the most part, *some strong quality in the mind, answering to and bringing out some new and striking quality in nature.*" The essence of genius, then, is originality in the sense of totally new creation or of the fresh reshaping and recharging of the experience of others. Hazlitt set up a contrast between the Neoclassic ideal of reason or judgment and the emerging Romantic concept of genius, between spontaneity and naturalness on the one hand and correctness and artificiality on the other. To a great extent the man of genius acts unconsciously. He is not merely one with great intellectual capacity which needs development; capacity and genius are totally different, with the former relating to quantity of knowledge and the latter to the source and quality. With a typically Romantic emphasis on the subjective and original he contended that "A retentive memory, a clear understanding is capacity, but it is not genius. . . . There is no place for genius but in the indefinite and unknown. . . . He is a man of capacity who possesses considerable intellectual riches: he is a man of genius who finds out a vein of new ore."

In no sense does the originality and exuberance associated with genius imply mere self-expression or, even worse, carelessness. Recognizing that the simple expression of individual feeling is easy and that much of the poetry of his contemporaries "is an experiment to reduce poetry to a mere effusion of natural sensibility," he grounded his idea of genius in "intense sympathy with some one beauty or distinguishing characteristic in nature," and strongly held that "wherever there is true genius, there will be true labour, that is, the exertion of that genius in the field most proper for it." Nor is genius a progressive phenomenon as each age builds on the achievements of the past. Hazlitt took a particular and distinctive stand on the problem of the "burden of the past" and the "anxiety of influence" written about so perceptively and movingly in recent years by W. J. Bate and Harold Bloom. Genius is not progressive, he argued, because it is not mechanical or definite or reducible to rule as science is. Genius loses more than it gains by transmission, and when the original inspiration has departed, "all the attempts to recal it are no better than the tricks of galvanism to restore the dead to life. The arts may be said to resemble Antæus in his struggle with Hercules, who was strangled when he was raised above the ground, and only revived and recovered his strength when he touched his mother earth."

Homer, Chaucer, Spenser, Shakespeare, Dante, Ariosto, Raphael, Titian, Michelangelo, Correggio, Cervantes, Boccaccio—these and other true geniuses lived at the dawn of their arts, and yet they generated them and brought them to magnificent levels of perfection. They were not, as much Neoclassic criticism dealt with them, diamonds in the rough, untutored and formless geniuses who manifest wit without judgment, beauty without art. Milton, almost alone among artists of later ages, seems to belong in their company. There have been great artists in the later ages of polish and cultivation—Hazlitt cites Tasso and Pope, Guido and Vandyke—but they were inferior to the almost divine originality and massive strength and vision of the great pioneers.

In a very real sense Hazlitt's brilliant conception of the creative and sympathetic imagination, his dynamic concept of genius, his persistent quest for originality were key features of the growing Romantic critical spirit of his time. If man's emotions are good and trustworthy when rooted in the grand and worthy objects of nature, the ideal course to follow was to express these emotions through the imagination's power to find their analogues in nature. The man of real genius "has the feeling of truth already shrined in his own breast, and his eye is still bent on nature to see how she expresses herself." Therefore, he argued, the poet of genius should pay less attention to rules, traditions, and customs, and look into his own heart and write. Insofar as the poet does this, his art gains originality and uniqueness, and with Hazlitt, as with a growing number of early nineteenth-century critics, these values increasingly became the focus of literary criticism.

DAVID BROMWICH

The Egotistical Sublime:
Wordsworth and Rousseau

Wordsworth, chastened by the reign of terror in France, and returning
to swell the war-whoop in England, came to exemplify all that Hazlitt most
distrusted about "poetic versatility" and the imagination's affinity for power;
and Hazlitt left a full record of those satiric epiphanies which cooled his
distrust into loathing: digressions on the spirit of poetry, and its opposition
to the spirit of humanity, that reach their climax in the years 1815–1820
in articles written for the *Examiner*. As he opened his lecture on "the living
poets" his audience must have expected the worst. And yet, Hazlitt began
it by praising Wordsworth as "the most original poet now living." He has
"produced a deeper impression, and on a smaller circle, than any other poet
in modern times has done, or attempted": modern times, for Hazlitt, would
have included every poet from Pope onward; and apart from the restriction,
on a smaller circle, he admits only one reservation. Wordsworth "cannot form
a whole." So in *The Excursion*, in spite of "noble materials . . . the poem
stands stock-still." The general application of this criticism to Wordsworth's
genius he explains by observing that Wordsworth "is totally deficient in all
the machinery of poetry." He then quotes all of "Hart-Leap Well," with
the warning, right for an interested propagandist who must be willing to
bully a little, that "those who do not feel the beauty and the force of it,
may save themselves the trouble of inquiring farther."

Only after all this does Hazlitt adopt the derisive nickname, "the Lake
school," which had been invented by reviewers as a tax on the efforts of
mutual promotion by Wordsworth, Southey, and Coleridge.

From *Hazlitt: The Mind of a Critic*. © 1983 by Oxford University Press. Originally entitled
"The Egotistical Sublime."

> A thorough adept in this school of poetry and philanthropy is jealous of all excellence but his own. He does not even like to share his reputation with his subject. . . . He tolerates only what he himself creates; he sympathizes only with what can enter into no competition with him, with "the bare trees and mountains bare, and grass in the green field." He sees nothing but himself and the universe. He hates all greatness and all pretensions to it, whether well or ill-founded. His egotism is in some respects a madness; for he scorns even the admiration of himself, thinking it a presumption in any one to suppose that he has taste or sense enough to understand him.

There follows an impressive list of Wordsworth's dislikes, including "all science and all art," everything from Voltaire and Newton to "conchology" and "the dialogues in Shakespeare." This is the part of Hazlitt's lecture that is usually remembered. But if he meant to advertise the power of Wordsworth's achievement as a thing attained in spite of egotism, the choice of "Hart-Leap Well" was subversive of his design. For the poem is a subtle instance of the appropriation by an egotistical poet of a subject he seems to hold at a distance—a demonstration of just how Wordsworth refuses "to share his reputation with his subject," and makes us admire him for refusing.

   "Hart-Leap Well" is written for more than one voice; and Hazlitt, who was a skilled performer of verse, would have impressed it on his audience that the voice which emerges at the end is Wordsworth's own.

> The pleasure-house is dust:—behind, before,
>   This is no common waste, no common gloom;
> But Nature, in due course of time, once more
>   Shall here put on her beauty and her bloom.
>
> She leaves these objects to a slow decay,
>   That what we are, and have been, may be known;
> But at the coming of the milder day,
>   These monuments shall all be overgrown.
>
> One lesson, Shpeherd, let us two divide,
>   Taught both by what she shews, and what conceals,
> Never to blend our pleasure or our pride
>   With sorrow of the meanest things that feels.

   The story is of a knight who builds a pleasure-house to commemorate his successful hunt for the "gallant brute" that died by the well. But the telling is elliptical; only the Shepherd's later embellishments complete it;

and only with the arrival of a third presence on the scene, Wordsworth's own, do the story and the ruins take on their proper meaning: nature has destroyed the pleasure house by "slow decay," to rebuke man's restless impulse to mingle his own pleasure and pride with the suffering of meanest things. The durability of momuments, a reader of Wordsworth may suppose, is conquered by the durability of human sympathies. True enough, Hazlitt replies by his choice of poems, but the means employed to perfect this moral are egotistical. The subject, the story, are nothing: they try to give an account of themselves but remain inarticulate until Wordsworth speaks for them.

Thus, in the *Lectures*, Hazlitt concedes the power of Wordsworth's egotism only by indirection. Elsewhere he makes the concession allegorically, by imputing to Rousseau certain qualities that seemed to him equally prominent in Wordsworth. But in a single plain sentence Hazlitt himself gives us the license for this easy transition: "we see no other sort of difference between them, than that the one wrote in prose and the other in poetry." Owing to distance of several kinds, Hazlitt was able to praise Rousseau with a warmth that never entered his tone in writing of Wordsworth: if politics made it hard for him to acknowledge Wordsworth's greatness, he could go on about Rousseau's, and allow no sort of difference between the genius of their works; the reader might draw his own inferences. Yet he portrayed Rousseau from several points of view, not all of them sympathetic. A representative sample of these may lend perspective to the less openly expressed shifts in his attitude toward Wordsworth. But the passages I will be quoting illustrate not the development of a single view but the constant revision and integration of more than one. As is often the case with Hazlitt, the conclusive judgments, offered at different stages of his life, contradict without appearing to exclude each other.

I begin with a little known passage from the review of Sismondi's *De la Litterature du Midi de L'Europe*, the second of Hazlitt's contributions to the *Edinburgh Review*. Whoever, he suggests, will compare the beauty of the young woman shrouded in her bower and listening to the song of the nightingale, in Chaucer's "The Flower and the Leaf," 'with a similar passage in Rousseau, the description of the Elysée in *La Nouvelle Héloïse*, may see how far the self-consciousness of the modern writer has impaired even his powers of observation. For the comparison shows

> the difference between good writing and fine writing; or between
> the actual appearances of nature and the progress of the feelings
> they excite in us, and a parcel of words, images and sentiments

thrown together without meaning or coherence. We do not
say this from any feeling of disrespect to Rousseau, for whom
we have a great affection; but his imagination was not that of
the poet or the painter. Severity and boldness are the characteristics of the natural style; the artificial is equally servile and
ostentatious.

Nothing is said in favor of the artificial style; it has only the fineness of
finery. Still, "we have a great affection" for Rousseau. So far the causes of
his affection are as obscure as his motive would be for thinking Wordsworth
original, had the reader been shown nothing but the satirical comment on
the Lake poets.

A more balanced judgment may be found in the "Character of Rousseau," which matches praise and blame as subtly as the Wordsworth lecture.

> His genius was the effect of his temperament. He created nothing,
> he demonstrated nothing, by a pure effort of the understanding.
> His fictitious characters are modifications of his own being, re-
> flections and shadows of himself. His speculations are the obvious
> exaggerations of a mind, giving loose to its habitual impulses,
> and moulding all nature to its own purposes. Hence his enthu-
> siasm and his eloquence, bearing down all opposition. Hence the
> warmth and the luxuriance, as well as the sameness of his de-
> scriptions. Hence the frequent verboseness of his style; for passion
> lends force and reality to language, and makes words supply the
> place of imagination. Hence the tenaciousness of his logic, the
> acuteness of his observations, the refinement and the inconsistency
> of his reasoning. . . . Hence his excessive egotism, which filled
> all objects with himself, and would have occupied the universe
> with his smallest interest.

"Passion" has now become Rousseau's element, and his whole justification.
While his singularity is perhaps to be regretted there is also something
admirable in it. He is a self-sympathizer; but within the limits of his exclusive
mode of feeling, we cannot doubt his sincerity, or persuade ourselves to
resist his spell. Everything he tells us is colored by the exaggerating power
of a mind turned in upon itself, yet for Hazlitt the imagination is necessarily
an exaggerating faculty; so Rousseau's failure to accomplish anything "by a
pure effort of the understanding" serves only to recommend him to those
who care for something more than understanding; and it is just such readers
Hazlitt has been courting, or hoping to create, in all his essays for *The Round*

Table. Rousseau substitutes words for things, but his words become our things, so long as we are reading him. His passion, concentrated as it is, cannot help being infectious. Hazlitt recognizes the danger that in the process reason may be made a pander to the will (in this case the will of the writer). He qualifies his enthusiasm accordingly, without altering his conviction that "passion," so far as it refuses to act in the service of petty self-interest, is an unmixed good no matter how egotistical its origins.

Sometimes he prefers to admit no qualification at all. Throughout his rhapsody on the march of intellect, in the sixteenth of his *Conversations of Northcote*, one feels that egotism has become his ally against a common enemy—power, "turretted, crowned, and crested"—and for this contest, the egotistical imagination is assimilated to a new and *principled* freedom. The march of course leads to the French Revolution, and egotism is the weapon every soldier has been issued along the way. With a pride unusual in these conversations, Hazlitt acknowledges the speech as his own, and climbs swiftly to the defiance of its liberating questions: to abridge him here would be unthinkable.

> Before we can take an author entirely to our bosoms, he must be another self; and he cannot be this, if he is "not one, but all mankind's epitome." It was this which gave such an effect to Rousseau's writings, that he stamped his own character and the image of his self-love on the public mind—*there* it is, and there it will remain in spite of every thing. Had he possessed more comprehension of thought or feeling, it would only have diverted him from his object. But it was the excess of his egotism and his utter blindness to every thing else, that found a corresponding sympathy in the conscious feelings of every human breast, and shattered to pieces the pride of rank and circumstance by the pride of internal worth or upstart pretension. When Rousseau stood behind the chair of the master of the *château* of ————, and smiled to hear the company dispute about the meaning of the motto of the arms of the family, which he alone knew, and stumbled as he handed the glass of wine to his young mistress, and fancied she coloured at being waited upon by so learned a young footman—then was first kindled that spark which can never be quenched, then was formed the germ of that strong conviction of the disparity between the badge on his shoulder and the aspirations of his soul—the determination, in short, that external situation and advantages are but the mask, and that the

mind is the man—armed with which, impenetrable, incorrigible, he went forth conquering and to conquer, and overthrew the monarchy of France and the hierarchies of the earth. Till then, birth and wealth and power were all in all, though but the framework or crust that envelopes the man; and what there was in the man himself was never asked, or was scorned and forgot. And while all was dark and groveling within, while knowledge either did not exist or was confined to a few, while material power and advantages were every thing, this was naturally to be expected. But with the increase and diffusion of knowledge, this state of things must sooner or later cease; and Rousseau was the first who held the torch (lighted at the never-dying fire in his own bosom) to the hidden chambers of the mind of man—like another Prometheus, breathed into his nostrils the breath of a new and intellectual life, enraging the Gods of the earth, and made him feel what is due to himself and his fellows. Before, physical force was every thing: henceforward, mind, thought, feeling was a new element—a fourth estate in society. What! shall a man have read Dante and Ariosto, and be none the better for it? Shall he be still judged of only by his coat, the number of his servants in livery, the house over his head? While poverty meant ignorance, that was necessarily the case; but the world of books overturns the world of things, and establishes a new balance of power and scale of estimation. Shall we think only rank and pedigree divine, when we have music, poetry, and painting within us? Tut! we have read *Old Mortality*; and shall it be asked whether we have done so in a garret or a palace, in a carriage or on foot? Or knowing them, shall we not revere the mighty heirs of fame, and respect ourselves for knowing and honouring them? This is the true march of intellect, and not the erection of *Mechanics' Institutions*, or the printing of *twopenny trash*, according to my notion of the matter, though I have nothing to say against them neither.

By the end of this speech, all Hazlitt's doubts about egotism seem to have vanished. Any author whom we love *must* be another self. Besides, Rousseau's want of comprehension now looks like a virtue, since anything less single-minded than the exclusive idea of himself would only have diverted him from his object—an object that is the greatest imaginable for any human mind, the discovery of "a corresponding sympathy" in the minds of others.

By that sympathy the world of books overturns the world of things. If we ask why the power of egotism, instead of merely teaching by example and so producing more egotism, now draws out a corresponding sympathy in the reader, the answer is that it is only with the egotism of another person that we sympathize in any case: we cannot sympathize with his sympathy. Rousseau overthrew "all the hierarchies" when he made inward feeling the measure of anyone's worth, and did so from the unshakable conviction of his own. Hazlitt's familiar image of the lamp of nature appears once again, but now as the Promethean fire kindled by man's imagination of himself, and kept alive by his ability to repose on the strength of his own aspirations. The triumph of words over things, and of the individual over the arbitrary power of despotism, is thus implicit in Rousseau's use of egotism. He sought and found a sympathetic response to the confessed privacy of his experience. After that, the march of intellect could not be stopped.

So far has Hazlitt come, with all he implies about the egotistical imagination in his lecture on Wordsworth and the associated remarks on Rousseau, that the distinction between the imagination's repose on nature and its repose on itself can no longer be maintained: the movement is exactly parallel to that of "Why the Arts are not Progressive?" Of course, "nature" may still be a useful slogan to combat the intrusions into poetry of a preening fashionability; and we may prefer the dramatic mode, and regard Shakespeare as somehow beyond all challenge. Yet if we are asked to account for the power of Shakespeare's poetry, we must resort to the same explanation that serves us in accounting for the power of Milton's or Wordsworth's: we can only say, Wordsworth looked into himself; Milton looked into himself; Shakespeare looked into himself. This extended movement of Hazlitt's thought can be summed up by saying that an unidealizing view of the imagination rescues from complete pessimism his unidealizing view of progress in the arts. If the history of art is mostly a history of diminishing returns, that is because the example of the great dead presses down on the memory of the living; yet tradition has no more determining force in the life of a poet than do "habitual trains of thought" in the life of a moral agent; we can never be sure when, by an act of vivid imagining, some one may not succeed in revising the precedents that define him. There are times for Hazlitt—looking at the Immortality Ode or "Michael," and comparing it with *The Rape of the Lock*—when he can regard even Wordsworth in this light.

This may be an unduly hopeful note on which to part from some of the gloomier pages bequeathed to us by nineteenth-century criticism. It will make a sufficiently dry conclusion to point out that the loss and gain entailed on literary history by Hazlitt's analysis have emerged with equal probability from a coherent idea of genius. Rhetorically he urges the claim of the "natural" or sympathetic artist. But he knows that this sort of genius differs from the egotist only in his choice of strategy, never in the work his imagination performs. The strengths of art are to be cherished for themselves, because they draw from each other by strange additions and none can offer a promise of transcending history. Hazlitt's tolerance would stand less in need of apology if it were a commoner trait among critics.

"Talent," one reader of Hazlitt has reminded us, "may frolic and juggle; genius realizes and adds." It was the talent rather than the genius for egotism that Hazlitt distrusted above all: the swagger of the man with a knack. That quality, with something too of a morbid restiveness which played havoc with the juggler's reflexes, he detected in Byron from his first reading of *Childe Harold's Pilgrimage*; and after quoting the stanzas in the fourth canto which describe the falls of Velino, he remarked: "There is here in every line an effort at brilliancy, and a successful effort; and yet, in the next, as if nothing had been tried, the same thing is attempted to be expressed again with the same labour as before, the same success, and with as little appearance of repose or satisfaction of mind." Once he had read a good many of the Waverley novels Hazlitt liked to set Byron against Scott, whose works showed invention, and the repose of a thousand truths in as many characters: in *The Spirit of the Age* it would seem right to praise Scott simply by reeling off their names. This was repeating the contrast between Shakespeare and Wordsworth; and it is in the special sense I have explored that Hazlitt declares the secret of Scott's mastery in three words: "*absence of egotism.*" In fact, the case against Byron could be made out with more propriety than that against Wordsworth, since Byron had ventured much farther onto Shakespeare's ground. When we finish a play by Shakespeare, we feel that we have seen a piece of the earth; with Byron, it is a carefully wild exotic preserve, and on every tree the tag: "Imported from Byronland."

I think Hazlitt was projecting his final estimate of Byron's dramatic powers when he engaged with Jeffrey to review *Sardanapalus*. But the way to a satisfying conclusion has been blocked by Jeffrey himself, for the published review was absorbed into his works instead of Hazlitt's: it seems to have been one of those instances in which the editor revised a contribution so extensively that he came to think it his own. The following passage, however, I believe to be entirely Hazlitt's.

> Close the play, and we meet with [Hamlet] no more—neither
> in the author's other works, nor any where else. A common author

who had hit upon such a character, would have dragged it in at every turn, and worn it to very tatters. Sir John Falstaff, again, is a world of wit and humour in himself. But except in the two parts of Henry IV, there would have been no trace of such a being, had not the author been "ordered to continue him" in the Merry Wives of Windsor. He is not the least like Benedick, or Mercutio, or Sir Toby Belch, or any of the other witty and jovial personages of the same author—nor are they like each other. Othello is one of the most striking and powerful inventions on the stage. But when the play closes, we hear no more of him. The poet's creation comes no more to life again, under a fictitious name, than the real man would have done. Lord Byron in Shakespeare's place, would have peopled the world with black Othellos! What indications are there of Lear in any of his [other] plays? . . . None. It might have been written by any other man, he is so little conscious of it. He never once returns to that huge sea of sorrow; but has left it standing by itself, shoreless and unapproachable.

There is, among other qualities, a prodigality in genius, a self-forgetfulness that sometimes looks like forgetfulness. The object of the poet's gaze is interesting while it interests him: it can be taken up with the sudden and transfiguring intensity that Hazlitt called "gusto" only because the poet knows that once put away, or overlooked, it may never again pass before him.

THE EXCURSION

Hazlitt's most substantial consideration of Wordsworth's poetry was his review of The Excursion, which appeared in three installments in The Examiner, between August 21 and October 2, 1814. It was the first serious discussion of Wordsworth's poetry by a critic who could claim to be neither an advocate set up by the poet himself nor a spokesman for fashionable literature. Jeffrey, whose article for the Edinburgh Review appeared a month later, for all his acuteness still wrote as a critic of the latter sort: every student of the period knows his opening line, "This will never do," and the tone of efficient scrupulosity that goes with it. Such is the tone that has dominated the intellectual journalism of the past one hundred fifty years. Yet Jeffrey's review appeals to no standard more exacting than the reader's expectation that he shall be entertained. Hazlitt's review, on the contrary, begins by granting that Wordsworth's poetry is something new in the world. And it was Hazlitt's review, far more than Coleridge's discussion of Wordsworth in the *Biographia Literaria*, which showed the first generation of readers *what* was new about the poetry.

Wordsworth himself seems to have understood the importance of Hazlitt in this respect, though his resentment in the end outweighed his gratitude: *Hazlitt, a younger man whom he knew*, had dared to speak of him critically. An anecdote, not yet canonical, about Wordsworth's reading aloud of the review, may be worth repeating here. Hazlitt tells it in the "Reply to Z," and must have heard the details through the *Blackwood's* critic John Wilson, who was with Wordsworth at the time. A critic for the *Examiner* might have been relied on to deprecate the poem on political ground alone, and, by his high-handedness both within literary society and without, Wordsworth had supplied certain of the contributors with a more personal reason for aversion. He would therefore have been anxious at the prospect of any report on the poem from that quarter—but let Hazlitt tell the story.

> Some time in the latter end of the year 1814 Mr. Wordsworth received an *Examiner* by the post, which annoyed him exceedingly both on account of the expence and the paper. "Why did they send that rascally paper to him, and make him pay for it?" Mr. Wordsworth is tenacious of his principles and not less so of his purse. "Oh," said Wilson, "let us see what there is in it. I dare say they have not sent it you for nothing. Why here, there's a criticism upon the Excursion in it." This made the poet (*par excellence*) rage and fret the more. "What did they know about his poetry? What could they know about it? It was presumption in the highest degree for these cockney writers to pretend to criticise a Lake poet." "Well," says the other, "at any rate let us read it." So he began. The article was much in favour of the poet and the poem. As the reading proceeded, "Ha," said Mr. Wordsworth, somewhat appeased, "there's some sense in this fellow too: the Dog writes strong." Upon which Mr. Wilson was encouraged to proceed still farther with the encomium, and Mr. Wordsworth continued his approbation; "Upon my word very judicious, very well indeed." At length, growing vain with his own and the *Examiner's* applause, he suddenly seized the paper into his own hands, and saying "Let me read it, Mr. Wilson," did so with an audible voice and appropriate gesture to the end, when he exclaimed, "Very well written indeed, Sir, I did not

expect a thing of this kind," and strutting up and down the room in high good humour kept every now and then wondering who could be the author, "he had no idea, and should like very much to know to whom he was indebted for such pointed and judicious praise"—when Mr. Wilson interrupting him with saying, "Oh don't you know; it's Hazlitt, to be sure, there are his initials to it," threw our poor philosopher into a greater rage than ever, and a fit of outrageous incredulity to think that he should be indebted for the first favourable account that had ever appeared of any work he had ever written to a person on whom he had conferred such great and unmerited obligations.

Only the first installment of the "Character of Mr. Wordsworth's New Poem, The Excursion" could have struck Wordsworth as very favorable. But for us the difficulty of recovering the whole feeling of the review is aggravated by the many revisions Hazlitt made before allowing it to be printed in *The Round Table*; these were done several months later, and by then he had doubtless heard of, and otherwise felt reverberations from, Wordsworth's reception of the piece; he had seen, too, the vindictiveness of Wordsworth's odes against Napoleon, which though they might seem to follow naturally from the political retreat of *The Excursion*, no critic could have predicted solely on the evidence of that poem. The paragraph on Wordsworth's politics, however, Hazlitt left as it stood. What he reworked for *The Round Table* was his tone, in the light of subsequent doubts concerning Wordsworth's politics and pastoralism: without actually strengthening these, Hazlitt makes them a good deal more prominent.

He accomplished the revision both by verbal changes and logical transpositions. In the *Examiner* he had regretted Wordsworth's pretence of story-telling, and wished he could have "given to his work the form of a philosophic poem altogether": in *The Round Table*, "philosophic" has become "didactic." Again, he had tried to convey the limitations of Wordsworth's poetry by distinguishing between imagination and sentiment, between "richness of invention and depth of feeling." The greatest poets have both; Young and Cowley have imagination or fancy, with too little of the common sentiments of mankind; while Wordsworth is preeminently the poet of feeling without invention. But a long passage introducing these categories is omitted from *The Round Table*, so that Hazlitt may circumscribe Wordsworth's genius more thoroughly. Where he wrote that Wordsworth's "imagination broods over that which is 'without form and void,' and 'makes it pregnant' "— plainly introducing a comparison with Milton—he now omits "imagination" in favor of "understanding," and thus implies the question: "What troubles will beset a long poem written in the age of Locke?" Even more decisive is the reframing of his conclusion. The last sentence in the *Examiner* had been: "It is not in our power to add to, or take away from, the pretensions of a poem like the present, but if our opinion or wishes could have the least weight, we would take our leave of it by saying—*Esto perpetua*!" The new conclusion for *The Round Table* comes from the first paragraph in the *Examiner*; and taken not as a qualification when praise is understood to follow, but as a summing-up when all praise is done, its effect is severe.

> If the skill with which the poet had chosen his materials had been equal to the power which he has undeniably exerted over them, if the objects (whether persons or things) which he makes use of as the vehicle of his sentiments, had been such as to convey them in all their depth and force, then the production before us might indeed "have proved a monument," as he himself wishes it, worthy of the author, and of his country. Whether, as it is, this very original and powerful performance may not rather remain like one of those stupendous but half-finished structures, which have been suffered to moulder into decay, because the cost and labour attending them exceeded their use or beauty, we feel that it would be presumptuous in us to determine.

By assigning his doubts a determinate position at the end of the review, Hazlitt did an injustice to the spirit in which he had conceived it. For this reason among others the earlier version seems to me preferable, and I shall be quoting it without further reference to *The Round Table*.

A challenge is laid down in the opening sentence which the rest of the review must try to meet: "In power of intellect, in lofty conception, in the depth of feeling, at once simple and sublime, which pervades every part of it and which gives to every object an almost preternatural and preterhuman interest, this work has seldom been surpassed." This is Longinian praise, yet we feel a remoteness from our sympathies in an interest "almost preternatural and preterhuman." By going on to describe the mountain landscape in which Wordsworth moves by elective affinity, Hazlitt tells us how a work that is cold to the touch may be great.

> The Poem of the *Excursion* resembles the country in which the scene is laid. It has the same vastness and magnificence, with the same nakedness and confusion. It has the same overwhelming, oppressive power. It excites or recals the same sensations which

those who have traversed that wonderful scenery must have felt. We are surrounded with the constant sense and superstitious awe of the collective power of matter, of the gigantic and eternal forms of Nature, on which, from the beginning of time, the hand of man has made no impression. Here are no dotted lines, no hedge-row beauties, no box-tree borders, no gravel walks, no square mechanic enclosures. All is left loose and irregular in the rude chaos of aboriginal nature. . . . Such is the severe simplicity of Mr. Wordsworth's taste, that we doubt whether he would not reject a druidical temple, or time-hallowed ruin, as too modern and artificial for his purpose. He only familiarises himself or his readers with a stone, covered with lichens, which has slept in the same spot of ground from the creation of the world, or with the rocky fissure between two mountains caused by thunder, or with a cavern scooped out by the sea. His mind is, as it were, coeval with the primary forms of things, holds immediately from nature; and his imagination "owes no allegiance" but "to the elements."

At this distance we are struck by what Hazlitt's first readers could not easily have known—the extent to which he was reviewing not *The Excursion* but all of Wordsworth's poetry leading up to it. When for example he evokes those "gigantic and eternal forms" on which "the hand of man has made no impression," he is recalling Wordsworth's claim in the Preface to *Lyrical Ballads*, to have chosen subjects from rustic life "because in that condition the passions of men are incorporated with the beautiful and permanent forms of nature." So the entire Wordsworthian program for poetry receives a fairer hearing than might have been expected. And the imaginative power Hazlitt admits him to possess is, from one point of view, the greatest he would admit for any poet: among those primeval shapes Wordsworth discourses as freely, as unserviceably, as Satan stalking *his* subject in *his* Chaos. But there is also a suggestion of puritanical self-denial in the "severe simplicity" of Wordsworth's taste: the same faculty that keeps him to his regimen will understandably put others out of patience. Why should he not furnish us with livelier matter for so long a journey?

He might do so, if it were an excursion into the country. But Hazlitt says in effect: you may search all England and not find a place like this. In his opening metaphor the vehicle has finally displaced the tenor; nothing but Wordsworth's mind has quite this look. The main argument of the review begins only after Hazlitt has interpreted the country, and the peculiar virtues ascribed to it, as a fiction of the probable-but-impossible sort. Some of his objections are therefore delayed: only in the final installment do we get the passage beginning, "All country people hate each other. . . . There is nothing good to be had in the country, or, if there is, they will not give it to you." It continues splendidly and exorbitantly, a long-delayed revenge for the country-jilt episode; for at that point Hazlitt felt he could afford to widen the attack. The key phrase of the paragraph just quoted—"his mind . . . holds immediately from nature"—had already made his position clear, by indicating both the intensity and the limitations of Wordsworth's power.

From this phrase Hazlitt derives his interpration of the whole poem as a psychological romance. And since everything we know about the poet leads us to expect that his talk will be about politics, the intensity of nature-instruction comes to be a measure of the repression of politics. In observing the inward turn of Wordsworthian romance, Hazlitt stresses repeatedly what the poem is not, as if the exclusions were deliberate. He was convinced that they were, and would use his conviction later in the review to open up the subject of politics. But for the time being the issue is held in suspense.

> The *Excursion* may be considered as a philosophical pastoral poem—as a scholastic romance. It is less a poem on the country than on the love of the country. It is not so much a description of natural objects, as of the feelings associated with them, not an account of the manners of rural life, but the result of the Poet's reflections on it. He does not present the reader with a lively succession of images or incidents, but paints the outgoings of his own heart, the shapings of his own fancy. He may be said to create his own materials; his thoughts are his real subject. . . . He sees all things in his own mind; he contemplates effects in their causes, and passions in their principles. He hardly ever avails himself of striking subjects or remarkable combinations of events, but in general rejects them as interfering with the workings of his own mind, as disturbing the smooth, deep, majestic current of his own feelings. Thus his descriptions of natural scenery are not brought home distinctly to the naked eye by forms and circumstances, but every object is seen through the medium of innumerable recollections, is clothed with the haze of imagination like a glittering vapour, is obscured with the excess of glory, has the shadowy brightness of a waking dream. The object is lost in the sentiment, as sound in the multiplication of echoes.

The dangers of this situation to the poet himself emerge in the next paragraph: "An intense intellectual egotism swallows up every thing. . . . The power of his mind preys upon itself." Still, as we see Wordsworth's universe through his eyes, it hardly seems possible that we should wish to look elsewhere: without him it would remain for us so much inanimate matter. Wordsworth "may be said to create his own materials," he is original, and for Hazlitt that marks an end of our search. The attitude here may remind us of Johnson's in the *Life of Swift*—another work by a critic temperamentally allied to his subject, in writing about whom the critic betrays a severity of reproach in proportion to the acuteness of his self-knowledge. For both Johnson and Hazlitt, all objections are silenced by the praise of originality. Even the words, "He sees all things in his own mind," would have had a special force for Hazlitt, from their inversion in the "Character of Rousseau": "He sees himself in all things." Though he would later profess to find no essential difference between them, it appears from this contrast that Wordsworth alone has got the epigram right, and with it the sublime perspective of egotism. For Rousseau "No matter what he looks at, it is himself that he sees"; for Wordsworth: "He looks into himself, and there finds all of nature." This of course had also been Dryden's praise of Shakespeare, repeated with small modifications by Pope, Johnson, and Hazlitt. It shows how generous his view of Wordsworth could become, and how far in practice his worries about egotism could be suspended or made to seem only the worries one always has about poets.

Only once does Hazlitt describe the tedium of the poem in Jeffrey's style; but even here, the tone never slips into mere decorous impatience, and the objection takes into account the strangeness of Wordsworth's genius, as well as the use to which a "philosophic" age puts all poetic gifts. Most of the passage was omitted from *The Round Table*, but it anticipates, more nearly than anything else in Hazlitt's first decade of journalism, the treatment of both Wordsworth and Coleridge in *The Spirit of the Age*.

> There is in his general sentiment and reflections on human life a depth, an originality, a truth, a beauty, and grandeur, both of conception and expression, which place him decidedly at the head of the poets of the present day, or rather which place him in a totally distinct class of excellence. But he has chosen to encumber himself with a load of narrative and description, which, instead of assisting, hinders the progress and effect of the general reasoning. Almost all this part of the work, which Mr. Wordsworth has inwoven with the text, would have come in better in plain

prose as notes at the end. Indeed, there is something evidently inconsistent, upon his own principles, in the construction of the poem. For he professes, in these ambiguous illustrations, to avoid all that is striking or extraordinary—all that can raise the imagination or affect the passions—all that is not every way common, and necessarily included in the natural workings of the passions in all minds and in all circumstances. Then why introduce particular illustrations at all, which add nothing to the force of the general truth, which hang as a dead weight upon the imagination, which degrade the thought and weaken the sentiment, and the connection of which with the general principle it is more difficult to find out than to understand the general principle itself? It is only by an extreme process of abstraction that it is often possible to trace the operation of the general law in the particular illustration, yet it is to supply the defect of abstraction that the illustration is given.

To acquit Hazlitt of any charge of complicity with *Edinburgh* taste, one need only compare the nuance of these lines with the self-possessing flippancy of Jeffrey as he frames an apparently similar complaint: "What Mr. Wordsworth's ideas of length are, we have no means of accurately judging; but we cannot help suspecting that they are liberal, to a degree that will alarm the weakness of most modern readers." As Jeffrey explains Wordsworth's autobiographical plan, the long poem of which *The Excursion* forms a part will cover the whole of Wordsworth's life up to the time when the poem was conceived, and "the quarto before us contains an account of one of his youthful rambles in the vales of Cumberland, and occupies precisely the period of three days; so that, by the use of a very powerful *calculus*, some estimate may be formed of the probable extent of the entire biography." It is a neat jibe, though frankly addressed to just that "weakness of most modern readers"—a weakness baffled by Spenser no less than Wordsworth—with which it affects to sympathize from an attitude of well-earned strength. Reduced to a single phrase, Hazlitt's paragraph also identifies a simple enough fault: "How much better it would be if he took out the plot, and then the characters!" But Hazlitt is saying something important about Wordsworth's ambivalent view of romance, and about the poem's elusiveness in relation to its declared genre. From his inmost moral being Wordsworth distrusts the *episode*, the "illustration"—all that dissolves the soul in pleasure, as Hazlitt said of *The Faerie Queene*, and holds it "captive in the chains of suspense"—so that as the narrator of several distinct stories he operates under constraint. He cannot bear to defer his moral, and yet morality is real to him only in its pure state, as exhortation. When we compare the illustrative tale with its parent truth we find that they are mismatched, or that any match would be improbable: they have wills of their own and prefer to stand alone. In *The Excursion* the two great impulses of romance, to tell a story and to give instruction, have thus separated out completely. Born an age too late, Wordsworth at every moment disappoints one of the aims his title had appeared to unite: excursus and excursion leave no room for each other.

"A single letter from the pen of Gray," Hazlitt says in an article written much later, "is worth all the pedlar-reasoning of Mr. Wordsworth's Eternal Recluse [the Wanderer], from the hour he first squats himself down in the sun to the end of his preaching. In the first we have the light unstudied pleasantries of a wit, and a man of feeling;—in the last we are talked to death by an arrogant old proser, and buried in a heap of the most perilous stuff and the most dusty philosophy." Hazlitt could think himself into such dismissals as easily as Jeffrey: but not when the poem was before him, and his duty was to present it to its first readers. His recognition of all Wordsworth's liabilities as a narrator leads him instead to question the narratability of Wordsworth's sort of poetry; and his conclusion is that the poem would have been more satisfying had it been more straightforwardly egotistical. In the end, therefore, Hazlitt says what his mind-landscape trope had only implied, that egotism is the wrong name for what troubles him in Wordsworth's poetry. Yet a look at a representative "illustration" may be necessary to explain his justification for sounding troubled at all.

The reader unfamiliar with *The Excursion* needs to be told here that its three main characters are the Wanderer, the Poet, and the Solitary: the first an old man who by slow accretions of experience has become a sage; the second a stand-in for Wordsworth, but several years younger than the author of the poem; the third a pretender-sage whose wisdom has been distorted by resentment, and whose experience is vexed by alternations of crisis and disappointment. The poem is a battle for the Solitary's soul, with everything in his own life conspiring to draw him into despair, and only the Wanderer fighting to redeem him. The contest has for its spectator one person, the Poet, and there are occasional suggestions that his great choices in life will be influenced by the outcome. What excitement the story possesses is owing to the self-doubt one imagines as a motive for the Poet's questions, and even for the answers supplied by the Solitary and the Wanderer. The three days' discourse, in nine books of about one thousand lines each, is varied beginning in Book V by the appearance of another character, a Pastor, whose function in the scheme of "Despondency" and "Despondency Corrected" is to administer routinely from tradition the comforts that the Wanderer has gathered and can impart through inspiration alone.

In Book VI the Pastor, walking among the gravestones of a mountain churchyard, recounts several of the histories they bring to mind. This survey appears to be mildly cautionary in intent: the cases he selects—a disappointed lover, a prodigal son, a pair of zealots, "flaming Jacobite / And sullen Hanoverian"—all illustrate some sort of restlessness of spirit being subdued to the love of nature and the uses of a community, even if this means a community of two. Against so exclusive a concern with those who have offered "obeisance to the world" the Solitary protests—too sharply, as Wordsworth informs us by temporarily renaming him the Skeptic, but still with a propriety that extends beyond this moment in *The Excursion*. He wonders why the destinies of those whom the community of men have cast out should not make equally fit matter for a tale, the more incumbent upon our sympathies because the more easily ignored. In saying this he has the sanction of Gray's Churchyard Elegy, and of Wordsworth in other places than *The Excursion*, so that he must be granted his eloquence.

> Say why
> That ancient story of Prometheus chained
> To the bare rock, on frozen Caucasus;
> The vulture, the inexhaustible repast
> Drawn from his vitals? Say what meant the woes
> By Tantalus entailed upon his race,
> And the dark sorrows of the line of Thebes?
> Fictions in form, but in their substance truths,
> Tremendous truths! familiar to the men
> Of long-past times, nor obsolete in ours.
> Exchange the shepherd's frock of native grey
> For robes with regal purple tinged; convert
> The crook into a sceptre; give the pomp
> Of circumstance; and there the tragic Muse
> Shall find apt subjects for her highest art.
>   (*Excursion*, VI, 538–552)

The Pastor is kept from such tales, of "grievous crimes / And strange disasters," by the constraints of his office; but the Poet now gives a different reason for passing them by, in keeping with Wordsworth's argument in the "Essay upon Epitaphs." A churchyard is a place where the memory of a community is preserved, and the record of each individual life is confirmed and given value by its association with others. If in rural districts the record is scant, this ought only to confirm the proper modesty of the storyteller. "Temptation here is none to exceed the truth. . . . And who can blame, / Who rather would not envy, men that feel / This mutual confidence; if from such source, / The practise flow,—if thence, or from a deep / And general humility in death?" About their own lives they are silent. Let us remember them therefore with the moral which the very presence of a graveyard seems to imply: we all go to the same end, and our last moments are necessarily moments of acceptance.

Grateful for this help, the Pastor affirms his intention to supply only such narratives as excite the genial affections; but he is not entirely satisfied with the Poet's reassurance, and confesses having felt a scruple about his own work as a moralist.

> And yet there are,
> I feel, good reasons why we should not leave
> Wholly untraced a more forbidding way.
> For, strength to persevere and to support,
> And energy to conquer and repel—
> These elements of virtue, that declare
> The native grandeur of the human soul—
> Are oft-times not unprofitably shown
> In the perverseness of a selfish course.
>   (*Excursion*, VI, 660–668)

The "more forbidding way" alludes, among other things, to the errant path of romance, in which the wanderer must be lost to be saved; the central lines of the passage, with their weird shift to the optative mood, register the dangers that lie in the way: the echo of Satan rousing his troops is very odd, and unless one has in mind Wordsworth's larger anxiety about the genre of the poem it can feel as if for the moment he had lost control.

The Pastor now points to the burial-place of a woman who even in death appears to refuse all connection with her neighbors. In life she was tall, dark, and saturnine, "surpassed by few / In power of mind, and eloquent discourse," with a serious and self-communing imagination, that required only the solitude of nature for support: indeed, in one of her characteristic attitudes, akin to the youthful Wordsworth—

> her head not raised to hold
> Converse with heaven, nor yet deprest towards earth,
> But in projection carried, as she walked
> For ever musing.
>   (*Excursion*, VI, 679–682)

But one aim of *The Excursion* is to make those elements of Wordsworth himself which correspond to the "Matron" here described, submit to a new control. So a strength that might be admirable in other settings—for example, a novel by George Eliot or Charlotte Brontë—is resolved into a peculiarly destructive compound of "ruling passions."

> Two passions, both degenerate, for they both
> Began in honour, gradually obtained
> Rule over her, and vexed her daily life;
> An unremitting, avaricious thrift;
> And a strange thraldom of maternal love,
> That held her spirit, in its own despite,
> Bound—by vexation, and regret, and scorn,
> Constrained forgiveness, and relenting vows,
> And tears, in pride suppressed, in shame concealed—
> To a poor dissolute Son, her only child.
>   *(Excursion*, VI, 706–715)

The marriage, we are told somewhat mysteriously, "opened with mishap," but there is no time for further explanations, because the life and this account of it both close suddenly. The Matron dies, "vexed and wrought upon" to the end, attended by her husband's sister, whose command of the household deepens her despair.

>   "And must she rule,"
> This was the death-doomed Woman heard to say
> In bitterness, "and must she rule and reign,
> Sole Mistress of this house, when I am gone?
> Tend what I tended, calling it her own!"
>   *(Excursion*, VI, 752–756)

By this time she has become more interesting to us than any inference Wordsworth can possibly draw from her way of life. A poet more settled in his task, Frost in "Home Burial," or Wordsworth in Book I of this poem, would let the picture answer for itself: but here the life must be grimly appraised, and tagged with its lesson. *She would not subdue herself to the conditions of life.* Yet we are told that the Pastor by happy accident, still on the right path, happened to pass near the window of her bedroom in the moments near her death; she looked at a shining star and was glad it would outlast her: this is then read back into the story as its clarifying episode, the much sought-for token of the Matron's acceptance of her human lot.

"With a sigh . . . yet, I believe, not unsustained / By faith in glory. . . .
She, who had rebelled, / Was into meekness softened and subdued."

Thus Wordsworth in pursuit of a moral. We know that the episode
interested Hazlitt since he quotes the lines about those tragedies that await
our discovery even in the humblest life. And in this instance we share his
bewilderment at illustrations, "the connection of which with the general
principle it is more difficult to find out than to understand the general
principle itself." Still, with the rest of the poem in view, and the gravity
of its concern for "Despondency Corrected," the moral of the Matron's
tragedy may easily enough be guessed. She withdrew herself from the life
and affections of a community, and Wordsworth, in response, would prefer
to have excluded her from the poem. He tells us so in the words of the
Poet, the character most nearly allied with himself. The Pastor by an extravagance of sympathy points out her gravestone nevertheless, and gives
her story, making the gesture of forgiveness which the Poet had hoped to
forestall. We are perhaps meant to treat the curious exchange as part of
Wordsworth's own education in charity; but the poem as a whole offers no
clear assurance on this score. In the end we may have to regard *The Excursion*
itself as one enormous "illustration," the connection of which with its own
moral remains uncertain throughout. For Wordsworth, who would teach
the good of community, can envision only a community that derives its
chief sustenance from those negative powers which ought to define but a
small part of its value: the power, for example, to exclude, or to withhold
sympathy from those it includes for the purpose of correction.

Yet the poem makes an honest picture of its uncertainties. The skeptical
and utopian arguments of the Solitary are allowed to emerge persuasively
enough for us to feel their intoxication, until we hear them answered by
the Wanderer; and even then, we may recall them vividly enough to suppose
that the Wanderer has the best of the debate only because his words are
always the last. Wordsworth seems to have felt so acutely the strength of
the Solitary's arguments that he took the trouble to discredit their advocate
beforehand, by exhibiting the unhappy life in which they took root, and to
which presumably they must always lead. So the most anxious moment of
the poem, for Wordsworth, and the most awkward for the reader, is the
moralized biography of the Solitary with which the Wanderer is kept busy
through the opening of Book II—interpreting the Village Wake he has
glimpsed from a distance as a sure sign of the Solitary's death; pronouncing
his eulogy with the mingled satisfaction and regret that befits the fulfillment
of a predictable fate; plucking the rain-drenched copy of Voltaire from the
mossy nook, and giving back a sermon on the desolation of a life parched

by skepticism. After that, the Solitary's refusal to be already dead is an anti-climax eight books long. To the reader it presents the constant irritation of any unresolved irony, though doubtless it was beyond the reach of Wordsworth's self-knowledge to have analyzed the Wanderer's motives for prematurely dismissing his friend into eternity.

In calling this an honest confusion and not just heartlessness, we adopt Hazlitt's insight: that *all* characters are really Wordsworth; but we must invent for ourselves the corollary: that Wordsworth is cruel to them in proportion as they bring to mind elements of himself which he now wants to banish. Certain characters, however, remain stubbornly attractive in spite of the narrator's disapproval, because too much was invested in them for Wordsworth to complete his task with the severity it required. At such moments as these, when the poet loses his moral claim on the reader, the pretence of drama vanishes and the poem has to be salvaged as a monologue broken arbitrarily into separate voices. Hazlitt's defense of Wordsworth starts from the need to apologize for just such moments; yet his review is a moral as well as a critical act, involving the recognition of a permanent dignity both in Wordsworth's isolation, and in the political ideals he had deserted. These emphases, both unexpected in 1814, were unimaginable in combination, and the excitement one can still feel about the review comes from seeing how they are brought together. In setting about his task Hazlitt took heart from the memory of comparable feats of generosity which he had seen performed by the Reverend Joseph Fawcett, a poet and lecturer of his father's generation, about whom he wrote in *The Life of Thomas Holcroft*: "He was one of the most enthusiastic admirers of the French Revolution; and I believe that the disappointment of the hopes he had cherished of the freedom and happiness of mankind, preyed upon his mind, and hastened his death." The description may remind us a good deal of Wordsworth's Solitary, for whom Fawcett was in fact generally taken to have been the model. Hazlitt would have had Fawcett often in his mind as he read the poem.

The dissent from Wordsworth's politics, to which Hazlitt devotes the second part of his review, is above all a protest against Wordsworth's portrait of the Solitary. Oppressed by private loss, as the Wanderer describes him—having seen his wife and two children die young and communed with their memory till he prayed for his own death—the Solitary is revived by the new and public energies of the French Revolution. But this "righteous cause," says the Wanderer, "Was served by rival advocates that came / From regions opposite as Heaven and Hell." Men like the Solitary, who confuse political design with personal compensation, will always demand most of their fellows and suffer the worst disappointments.

An overweening trust was raised; and fear
Cast out, alike of person and of thing.
Plague from this union spread, whose subtle bane
The strongest did not easily escape;
And He, what wonder! took a mortal taint.
How shall I trace the change, how bear to tell
That he broke faith with them whom he had laid
In the earth's dark chambers, with a Christian's hope!
An infidel contempt of holy writ
Stole by degrees upon his mind; and hence
Life, like that Roman Janus, double-faced;
Vilest hypocrisy—the laughing, gay
Hypocrisy, not leagued with fear, but pride.
                              (*Excursion*, II, 241–253)

In the passage that follows, the Wanderer's denunciation of the Solitary as an infidel cannot quite erase our impression that Wordsworth objects to his revolutionary zeal on different grounds altogether. What troubles Wordsworth is that the Solitary has dared to hope; in searching for a good beyond his sufferings he has somehow been false to them. That is the real meaning of "breaking faith" with the memory of his wife and children. However, for Wordsworth to interpret the story in this way would have meant giving up the political and religious debates, and admitting that his whole interest lay elsewhere. In choosing instead to speak through the Wanderer—sanctioned by a piety not his own—he found a license for the triumphant scorn with which he concludes his account of the Solitary's life. The words are not his, they are spoken by a man assured, as Wordsworth could not be, that *these* hopes were wrong to entertain: but even so we may feel there is something indecent in the tone.

The glory of the times fading away—
The splendour, which had given a festal air
To self-importance, hallowed it, and veiled
From his own sight—this gone, he forfeited
All joy in human nature; was consumed,
And vexed, and chafed, by levity and scorn,
And fruitless indignation; galled by pride;
Made desperate by contempt of men who throve
Before his sight in power or fame, and won,
Without desert, what he desired; weak men,
Too weak even for his envy or his hate!

> Tormented thus, after a wandering course
> Of discontent, and inwardly opprest
> With malady—in part, I fear, provoked
> By weariness of life—he fixed his home,
> Or, rather say, sate down by very chance,
> Among these rugged hills; where now he dwells,
> And wastes the sad remainder of his hours,
> Steeped in a self-indulging spleen, that wants not
> Its own voluptuousness;—on this resolved,
> With this content, that he will live and die
> Forgotten,—at safe distance from "a world
> Not moving to his mind."
>
> (*Excursion*, II, 293–315)

Those final phrases about the Solitary, with certain others later in the poem, that speak of his "one bare dwelling; one abode, no more," link him with a type of Wordsworthian character especially fit for redemption: Margaret for example, in the first book of *The Excursion*, dying in the place that has witnessed the death of her hopes, "Last human tenant of these ruined walls"; or Wordsworth in the "Elegiac Stanzas on Peele Castle," as he describes himself, "Housed in a dream, at distance from the Kind." But the general tendency of the passage is to find its subject easily deplorable. His conversion, we feel, would make an unendurable trial and had better be spared: to which end the Wanderer quickly moves by supposing him dead.

Let us see how far we can square Wordsworth's portrait of the Solitary with some passing remarks about Joseph Fawcett in Hazlitt's *Table-Talk* essay "On Criticism." The point of this exercise is to test Wordsworth's generosity to a rival, by which his claim to the title of dramatic poet must finally be judged.

> I have sometimes thought that the most acute and original-minded men made bad critics. They see every thing too much through a particular medium. . . . Men who have fewer native resources, and are obliged to apply oftener to the general stock, acquire by habit a greater aptitude in appreciating what they owe to others. . . . I might take this opportunity of observing, that the person of the most refined and least contracted taste I ever knew was the late Joseph Fawcett, the friend of my youth. He was almost the first literary acquaintance I ever made, and I think the most candid and unsophisticated. . . . "That is the most delicious feeling of all," I have heard him exclaim, "to like what

is excellent, no matter whose it is." In this respect he practised what he preached. He was incapable of harbouring a sinister motive, and judged only from what he felt. There was no flaw or mist in the clear mirror of his mind. . . . Most men's minds are to me like musical instruments out of tune. Touch a particular key, and it jars and makes harsh discord with our own. They like Gil Blas, but can see nothing to laugh at in Don Quixote: they adore Richardson, but are disgusted with Fielding. Fawcett had a taste accommodated to all these. He was not exceptious. He gave a cordial welcome to all sorts, provided they were the best in their kind. . . . A heartier friend or honester critic I never coped withal. He has made me feel (by contrast) the want of genuine sincerity and generous sentiment in some that I have listened to since, and convinced me (if proof were wanting) of the truth of that text of Scripture—"That had I all knowledge and could speak with the tongues of angels, yet without charity I were nothing!" I would rather be a man of disinterested taste and liberal feeling, to see and acknowledge truth and beauty wherever I found it, than a man of greater and more original genius, to hate, envy, and deny all excellence but my own—but that poor scanty pittance of it (compared with the whole) which I had myself produced!

For those who could see beyond the speeches to the man, Fawcett seemed the very pattern of a disinterested sympathy. Indeed it was Fawcett, as Hazlitt reminds us in another place, who bound the *Rights of Man* and *Reflections on the Revolution in France* into one volume, saying that together they made a good book. How then do we judge the poet who can see here only the fixities of the ideologue?

In one sense this is a false problem, for we need not suppose that Hazlitt and Wordsworth were describing the same man. But we have to remember that Hazlitt supposed they were; that he doubtless took the Solitary to represent what Wordsworth would have done with any man like Fawcett; and that these considerations entered into his thinking about the poem. In the review itself he was showing Wordsworth a Fawcett-like generosity. Instead of dwelling on Wordsworth's defects of sympathy, he would take the "best of that kind" of poetry, and interpret the Solitary as a partial portrait of Wordsworth. The whole poem would then become egotistical but great of its kind: the political sermons could be met head-on, having so to speak fallen out of solution, and no longer enjoying the protection of dramatic immunity. Years after writing the review, Hazlitt still cannot summon memories of Fawcett without setting him against Wordsworth; and in the paragraph I quoted from "On Criticism," he deploys the whole established arsenal of anti-egotistical tropes. The dense particular medium of Wordsworth's mind discovers its contrary in the unmisted mirror of Fawcett's. Again, as in the lecture-cadenza on the Lake poets, we are warned of the tendency in "original-minded men" to insist on some "exclusive excellence." A special irony is reserved for Wordsworth's pretensions as a sage, and this would touch most of all the Wordsworth of *The Excursion*: it is Fawcett, the figure of generous common sense, and not Wordsworth, the hoarder of a single interest raised to the intensity of genius, who can draw more often on what Hazlitt calls "the general stock" of ideas—that is, the ideas shared by a community. The implication is that men like Fawcett and not Wordsworth, men reluctant to discard even the most far-fetched vision of utopia as the wreckage of their youth, are likelier some day to advance from the "one abode, no more!" that houses poets and fanatics, and to form part of a living community.

Wordsworth's view of the Solitary provoked the most famous section of the review: Hazlitt's defense of the French Revolution. This has occasionally been dismissed as a fit of spleen. With the facts before us, however, we can now understand it as the final move in a well-pondered strategy. The question of Wordsworth's politics had been opened by his neglect of dramatic artifice: no author above the battle would have granted one of his characters the same liberty, and steady advantage in dealing with another, which the Wanderer evidently has in all his speeches to the Solitary. The speeches revolve around Wordsworth's twin ideals of concern and retreat— an unstable combination throughout his poetry, and never more so than here. As for the double piety which emerges, Hazlitt distrusts it from the bottom of his soul. He begins his denunciation by quoting the Wanderer's eloquent summary of the fate of the revolution. Lamenting the darkness that has "overspread / The groaning nations" in the bloody aftermath, together with "that other loss, / The loss of confidence in social man"—the Sage, as Wordsworth calls him throughout this part, admits nevertheless that by "faith more firm . . . the Bad / Have fairly earned a victory o'er the weak." Hazlitt's reply winds deliberately into its strength, and then as deliberately uncoils.

> In the application of these memorable lines, we should perhaps differ a little with Mr. Wordsworth; nor can we indulge with him in the fond conclusion afterwards hinted at, that one day

our triumph, the triumph of virtue and liberty, may be complete. For this purpose, we think several things necessary which are impossible. It is a consummation which cannot happen till the nature of things is changed, till the many become as the *one*, till romantic generosity shall be as common as gross selfishness, till reason shall have acquired the obstinate blindness of prejudice, till the love of power and of change shall no longer goad man on to restless action, till passion and will, hope and fear, love and hatred, and the objects to excite them, that is, alternate good and evil, shall no longer sway the bosoms and business of men. All things move not in progress, but in a ceaseless round; our strength lies in our weakness; our virtues are built on our vices; our faculties are as limited as our being; nor can we lift man above his nature more than above the earth he treads.

So far the modified hopes endorsed by the Wanderer have been accepted as solid sense, for they are in keeping with the *Essay on Human Action*, where Hazlitt admitted the common basis of good and evil actions. But in Wordsworth's injunction to choose, between the extremes of hope and despair, some "middle point, whereon to build / Sound expectations," he senses the deeper complacency of a man to whom many new oppressions will soon be thinkable. Hazlitt continues:

But though we cannot weave over again the airy, unsubstantial dream, which reason and experience have dispelled—

"What though the radiance which was once so bright
Be now for ever taken from our sight,
Though nothing can bring back the hour
Of glory in the grass, of splendour in the flower":—

yet we will never cease, nor be prevented from returning on the wings of imagination to that bright dream of our youth; that glad dawn of the day-star of liberty; that spring-time of the world, in which the hopes and expectations of the human race seemed opening in the same gay career with our own . . . when, to the retired and contemplative student, the prospects of human happiness and glory were seen ascending, like the steps of Jacob's ladder, in bright and never-ending succession. The dawn of that day was suddenly overcast; that season of hope is past; it is fled with the other dreams of our youth, which we cannot recal, but

has left behind it traces, which are not to be effaced by birthday odes, or the chaunting of *Te Deums* in all the churches of
Christendom. To those hopes eternal regrets are due; to those
who maliciously and wilfully blasted them, in the fear that they
might be accomplished, we feel no less what we owe—hatred
and scorn as lasting.

In tone this is very close to the peroration of Hazlitt's lecture "On the Living
Poets." The men now renouncing their early ideals once showed him the
prospects of happiness "like the steps of Jacob's ladder": the phrase, associated
in his mind with Coleridge's eloquence, reminds him in turn of a favorite
sentence from *La Nouvelle Héloïse*, which he would use again to introduce
"My first Acquaintance with Poets." "*Il y a des impressions que ni le temps ni
les circonstances peuvent effacer.*" Those words here find their echo in the suggestion of all that birthday-odes cannot efface. On the impulse of such
memories even the sounding numbers of Wordsworth's great elegy are
hitched into the lost cause, where for a moment, and without the lines that
follow, they seem rightly to belong.

The figurative movement of the passage reveals Hazlitt's usual gift for
a metaphysical skepticism and moral firmness which are sometimes supposed
to exclude each other. What remains of the cause, after all, is only one's
fidelity to the task of remembering. But it plays our memories false to
exclaim with Wordsworth: "By a curious sequence of events, too sad to
recount in their whole length, our fair seed-time was lost." There are, says
Hazlitt, for this as for other human actions, particular agents responsible
for the outcome. And they can be sought out, and punished, with words:
we must not from a pretended charity relax our love of truth. Thus, to
Wordsworth's nostalgia he opposes a narrower but more fully transitive quest
for vengeance. The gesture is crude by comparison, and derives its great
strength from its readiness to appear so. One may recall that Hazlitt when
sufficiently roused was not above the Junius-like tactic of confronting an
enemy with his grey hairs. Something almost as abrupt is happening here.
The ghost of Wordsworth's youth is visited upon the spectral impotence of
his middle age, and Hazlitt personally assures him that the visitations will
continue forever.

From much recent discussion of Wordsworth's poetry *The Excursion* has
been excluded altogether. And yet, by a consensus so complete that it need
never be articulated, we now recognize in Wordsworth's disenchantment
the single attitude by which a poet is likeliest to survive his own dealings
with politics, and to command our admiration in retrospect: the modern

critic who has not learned this from Yeats will have come to know it more obliquely from Eliot or Auden. The result has been an oddly uncritical acceptance of Wordsworth's position—in the work of his most scrupulous commentators, one can feel that he has survived Hazlitt's challenge almost uncontested. That *The Excursion* should be shelved in favor of *The Prelude* is of course nothing against the apology both poems advance. *The Prelude*, with its sufficiently confessional disclaimers, would in any case be more congenial to modern taste. But, to repeat, it was *The Excursion* alone that Hazlitt and other contemporaries had to refer to, in framing their response to Wordsworth's account of his own political conversion. And only one modern defense of Wordsworth, E. P. Thompson's "Disenchantment or Default: A Lay Sermon," has relied chiefly on *The Excursion*.

In that essay Thompson pointed out that Wordsworth could claim to have been disenchanted by certain experiences, of which he tried to make an honest record: the modern reader, in contrast, is apt to use the accumulated moral capital of Wordsworth's disenchantment as a means of dignifying his own unchanging complacency. Thompson writes as an admirer of both Hazlitt and Wordsworth, but in examining the passage just quoted he finds Hazlitt's rhetoric uncharacteristically strained. Perhaps, in 1814, *these* ideals could no longer summon a language proved on the pulses of feeling; perhaps that is why Hazlitt's "we will never cease" has an urgency the preceding words seem not to have earned. But Thompson also looks beyond Hazlitt, to a moment of history when the rhetorical gestures associated with any ideal whatever must similarly have faltered.

> How far is it possible for men to hold on to aspirations long after there appears to be no hope of inserting them into "the real world which is the world of all of us"? If the social context makes all insertion seem impossible—if all objective referents for these hopes are cruelly obliterated—if the attempt to live out the ideals appears to produce their opposite—if *fraternité* produces fratricide, *egalité* produces empire, liberty produces liberticide—then aspirations can only become a transposed interior faith. There may be a deepening of sensibility. But the dangers are also evident. This driving back into interior faith, this preoccupation with trying to "hold" and to meditate upon past states of feeling, is surely the clue not only to the increasingly self-preoccupied tone of Wordsworth's life, and style of life, as the Lake poet, but also to the increasing failure of *observation* even in his nature poetry. . . . If there is a moral, it is not that he became a poorer poet

because he changed his political views, but that his new "good views" were not held with the same intensity and authenticity.

With this context understood, Thompson wonders how far Hazlitt may have resigned himself to displaying his refusal of "transposed faith" as a willed act of defiance.

> How long could any man have stood a tension of that sort, at its full creative intensity, between a vision of the universal heart, and the marching and counter-marching of armies across Europe? There must be *some* objective referent for social hope, and it is one trick of the mind to latch on to an unworthy object in order to sustain such hope. Those who did not become apostates in this circle did not fare much better. Some, like James Losh, became cautious Whigs and exponents of the new political economy, whose cash equivalents opened up a distance between men immeasurably colder than that of Tory paternalism. Hazlitt preserved much of the early vision [in the passage quoted]. . . . But there is a curious arrest, a stasis, in this: the passage works by means of a tension between stale libertarian rhetoric ("glad dawn," "day-star," "golden era") pressed to the point of self-mockery, nostalgic rhythms, and sudden, muscular polemic. Hazlitt could maintain his affirmatives only by latching on to the hero figure of Napoleon, and by sustaining his aspiration out of a kind of whimsy fortified by rancor.

In the literature of two centuries Thompson's is the most eloquent and sympathetic attack on the politics of Hazlitt's criticism: but the object of the attack is partly his own invention; the doubts that he supposes Hazlitt felt, and repressed for the sake of this review, were never as strong as we may wish them to have been.

For all Hazlitt's profound distrust of political economy, he would never have admitted that it opened up a distance between men "immeasurably colder" than what came before—that warm and proper distance of which we hear so much in Wordsworth's revisions for Book I of *The Excursion*: "rosy" children, "homely" fare, "the keen, the wholesome, air of poverty," to repeat only the paternalistic tag-words cited by Thompson. If we nevertheless assume that Hazlitt in his self-counsels must have shared some part of Wordsworth's nostalgia, we do so from the perspective of the 1840s and of all we now know about the effects of the First Reform Bill. But here, though his causeries against utilitarianism have something even of the eloquence of *Hard Times*, Hazlitt must be allowed to be a very imperfect prophet. He did not guess that the retrospective politics of *The Excursion* might one day appear as an alternative vision of community to be cherished in good faith. And we can trace his failure to see this to a date much later than the review; indeed, to a comment from 1830. Hazlitt had asked Macvey Napier, Jeffrey's successor at the *Edinburgh*, to review Southey's *Colloquies*. The book as it turned out was given to Macaulay to review, and he did so in a style, and with comments on Southey's literary gifts, closely modeled on Hazlitt's treatment of him in *Political Essays*, *The Spirit of the Age*, and the *Edinburgh* article on Coleridge's *Biographia*. It was, however, not Macaulay's style alone but his unromantic *laissez-faire* politics that pleased Hazlitt as he read the review, with its dismissal of Southey's paternalism, and endorsement of "leaving capital to find its most lucrative course, commodities their fair price, industry and intelligence their natural reward, idleness and folly their natural punishment." With these phrases still in his ear Hazlitt could write to Napier: "I am not sorry I had not *Southey* as it is so ably done."

Now, Macaulay's engagement with the *Colloquies* is similar in kind to Hazlitt's with *The Excursion*, and in the more than fifteen years given him to modify his views Hazlitt has not retreated an inch. I agree with Thompson that it would be more satisfying to his admirers if he had; but as there is no evidence on the point, I think it wrong to suppose his protest against Wordsworth can be reduced to whimsy fortified by rancor; or that he might in other circumstances have said a word in favor of Wordsworth's nostalgia as a decent choice among poor alternatives. We must recall that Hazlitt was arguing with Wordsworth not only about Wordsworth's past but his own. He could renew the same rhetoric, its stale figures beautifully refreshed, in a later essay like "On the Feeling of Immortality in Youth," where he writes without the benefit of *The Prelude* (Book XI) but in a comparable strain.

> For my part, I set out in life with the French Revolution, and that event had considerable influence on my early feelings, as on those of others. Youth was then doubly such. It was the dawn of a new era, a new impulse had been given to men's minds, and the sun of Liberty rose upon the sun of Life in the same day, and both were proud to run their race together. Little did I dream, while my first hopes and wishes went hand in hand with those of the human race, that long before my eyes should close, that dawn would be overcast, and set once more in the night of despotism—"total eclipse!"

In a very different strain, he approaches as nearly Wordsworth's "daring sympathies with power," when he writes elsewhere that on hearing news of Napoleon's victory at Austerlitz, "I walked out in the afternoon, and, as I returned, saw the evening star set over a poor man's cottage with other thoughts and feelings than I shall ever have again."

Hazlitt, then, as he contemplated a long poem which aimed to change men's minds about politics no less than poetry, was confronting Wordsworth's past with his own. The political claims of *The Excursion*—which he takes to be isolable from its grandeur of conception and its power of interesting us in a single self—are first scattered from coherence with the rest of the poem, and only then discredited. I have already compared this with the much simpler strategy followed by Jeffrey. It may now be worth adding De Quincey to the comparison. After all, he wrote of the poem at some length, in his essay "On Wordsworth's Poetry," and from reposing greater trust in the exclusive demands of Wordsworth's imagination, might be expected to regard it more sympathetically. But in fact it seems to have caused him boundless irritation. He catches a glimpse of the moral ambiguities disclosed by Wordsworth's relation to the Wanderer, and has doubts about any character who can have "found so luxurious a pleasure in contemplating a pathetic *phthisis* of heart in the abandoned wife," but he quickly trivializes the issue by putting to the Wanderer the rhetorical question, "Pray, amongst your other experiments, did you ever try the effect of a guinea?", and at last is sidetracked into one of his appalling jokes. A report from a neighborhood coroner, he says, would have found that Margaret's child died chiefly of "sloth, and the habit of gadding about." It is beside such procedures as this that we come to value Hazlitt's undeviating seriousness. Nothing about the poem seems to him quaint or absurd. As for Wordsworth's politics, they are rejected not because they disagree with Hazlitt's, not because they have swerved from an ideal of progress—but because the revolutionary fraternity of the 1790s had been the only community Wordsworth ever lived in for long, by voluntary association; and now his strange choice of tactics, confessing bad motives in himself and inviting others to admit they shared them, has overturned Hazlitt's faith that he can fairly represent any community at all.

If Hazlitt had to resort to a language not quite his own in affirming the aims of a lost community, he could respond to Wordsworth's praise of an invented one with entirely characteristic vehemence. Indeed, for both Wordsworth and Hazlitt in this encounter, it is the negative moment of rhetorical performance, the *reprehensio*, which triumphs: Wordsworth on France is matched by Hazlitt on the country.

The common people in civilised countries are a kind of domes-
ticated savages. . . . They are taken out of a state of nature,
without being put in possession of the refinements of art. The
customs and institutions of society cramp their imaginations
without giving them knowledge. If the inhabitants of the moun-
tainous districts described by Mr. Wordsworth are less gross and
sensual than others, they are more selfish. Their egotism becomes
more concentrated, as they are more insulated, and their purposes
more inveterate, as they have less competition to struggle with.
The weight of matter which surrounds them, crushes the finer
sympathies. Their minds become hard and cold, like the rocks
which they cultivate. The immensity of their mountains makes
the human form appear little and insignificant. Men are seen
crawling between Heaven and earth, like insects to their graves.
Nor do they regard one another more than flies on a wall.

Hazlitt's opening gambit, that *The Excursion* "resembles the country in
which the scene is laid," looks different in the light of this conclusion. It
is tempting to split the difference, and say that the poem presents a country
of Wordsworth's imagining and the review a country of Hazlitt's: but that
concession itself does far more to stagger Wordsworth's pretensions than
Hazlitt's. For *The Excursion* is the poem in which Wordsworth steps forward
decisively to address us as the poet of ordinary life. This claim holds up very
well throughout the poem, largely owing to the way "The Ruined Cottage"
shelters the remaining eight books; so that De Quincey could chide Hazlitt
with some show of propriety, for contriving "the least plausible objection"
ever brought against Wordsworth's poetry in the sentence: "One would
suppose, from the tenor of [Wordsworth's] subjects, that on this earth there
was neither marrying nor giving in marriage." But in putting it this way,
all Hazlitt denies is that Wordsworth can make such actions as marriage—
such communications between me and my neighbor, such bonds uniting
mind with mind—actual to his readers with the force he commands in
making solitude actual, and the power of one mind in solitude. De Quincey's
strictures, it may be remarked, closely and rather surprisingly anticipate
Thompson's. He too wants to restore to Wordsworth something of the
dignity of his intentions in writing *The Excursion*. Hazlitt would have felt
a good deal of sympathy with these efforts at rehabilitation, but for him
the poet who expresses egotistical power, and the poet who represents the
affections of a community, cannot dwell in the same body at the same time.
He understands the depth at which the hope of fulfilling a double office has

been experienced; yet he sees that Wordsworth will never cease to prize the lustre of a personal glory above all.

What may be called the received figure of Wordsworth for the second half of the nineteenth century and the first several decades of the twentieth—the Wordsworth evoked for us by Arnold's touchstone line, "Of joy in widest commonalty spread"—this poet, at his first annunciation, seemed to Hazlitt a hollow thing. The essence of Wordsworth's genius he took to be a sublimity whose only true occasion could be a history of the self. The assurance with which he maintained that estimate brings him closer to Bradley, and his successors in our own day, than to any nineteenth-century critic of Wordsworth; and it accounts for the feeling we can sometimes have as we read him, that he has mistaken his text and by uncanny transposition found a way to review *The Prelude* before its time. Yet he negotiated his task while also fulfilling a journalistic duty—for which he neither felt nor expressed the slightest degree of contempt—the duty to serve his readers as a generous guide to the complexities of voice that make the chief difficulty of *The Excursion*. We ought to consider finally the sort of tact Hazlitt can impart for our reading of passages he does *not* discuss: one such instance is the Solitary's renunciation of life and the energies of life, which closes the book entitled "Despondency."

> The tenor
> Which my life holds, he readily may conceive
> Whoe'er hath stood to watch a mountain brook
> In some still passage of its course, and seen,
> Within the depths of its capacious breast,
> Inverted trees, rocks, clouds, and azure sky;
> And, on its glassy surface, speck of foam,
> And conglobated bubbles undissolved,
> Numerous as stars; that, by their onward lapse,
> Betray to sight the motion of the stream,
> Else imperceptible. Meanwhile, is heard
> A softened roar, or murmur; and the sound
> Though soothing, and the little floating isles
> Though beautiful, are both by Nature charged
> With the same pensive office; and make known
> Through what perplexing labyrinths, abrupt
> Precipitations, and untoward straits,
> The earth-born wanderer hath passed; and quickly,
> That respite o'er, like traverses and toils

> Must he again encounter.—Such a stream
> Is human Life; and so the Spirit fares
> In the best quiet to her course allowed;
> And such is mine,—save only for a hope
> That my particular current soon will reach
> The unfathomable gulf, where all is still!
> (*Excursion*, III, 967–991)

Without Hazlitt's aid we might hear in this only the lament of a materialism returning aridly on itself, and finding dearth in nature's sublimest scenes because it has brought nothing to them. What Hazlitt encourages us to hear besides, is how far these sentiments implicate Wordsworth himself, so that his own voice gives companionable relief to the Solitary's, and works for his vindication. The echoes of "Tintern Abbey," in the sound of the soft inland murmur, and of the Boy of Winander episode of *The Prelude*—in the concern for how reflection may procure or impede "Knowledge not purchased by the loss of power"—indeed indicate a closer kinship between poet and solitary than Wordsworth was prepared to acknowledge. Here as elsewhere Hazlitt testifies for the tale against the teller. And, so far as the passage and others like it, with their hints of what "perplexing labyrinths, abrupt / Precipitations, and untoward straits, / The earth-born wanderer hath passed," look forward to the romance of the egotistical sublime in *Alastor* and *Endymion*, Hazlitt has informed our sense of the connection, by all his doubts respecting the future of dramatic poetry. Of those doubts both his praise and blame of *The Excursion* were a fitting summation.

DAVID BROMWICH

The Politics of Allusion

QUOTATION AND ALLUSION

A critic when he quotes is interrupting the text to which his chosen passage belongs, and exhibiting his power in relation to an author he cares for, at the same time that he acknowledges the author's mastery over him. His wish is to take possession of what he was possessed by. No interesting act of quotation therefore can imply a simple gesture of homage; the reader cannot help being interested in more than the accuracy of the result. In quoting one summons both a witness and a judge to the "tribunal of the soul" which Longinus speaks of, where every writer hopes to be judged great by his sympathy with the great writers who preceded him. Whatever fragment the critic picks out for emphasis will distort its parent text by presenting less than the whole of it, and so will shape the reader's understanding of everything it does not mention. Longinus's definition of sublimity, as "the echo of a great soul," admits, only more openly than other phrases about literary invention, the distance between any great work and a vivid memory of it. The distance and the change it brings about are necessary to appreciation, because according to Longinus we are unwilling as well as unable, when we have been moved by a work of literature, to see it steadily and see it whole. Once that is recognized, it may be added that there evidently is such a thing as having a genius for quotation.

Hazlitt often quoted from memory. His favorite lines, including those his memory had changed, he exhibited with the tacit understanding that they were to be read not merely as evidence of conscientiousness, but as a

From *Hazlitt: The Mind of a Critic.* © 1983 by Oxford University Press.

leading clue to every quality that ought to be searched out in *his* writing. Quotation in this sense, judged as a critical tactic, marks the pride not the humility of the writer who quotes: "Here you see what I have found, what I remember, what I now prefer to think mine; part of my character—a great part of what makes me unique." De Quincey thought Hazlitt went too far in the direction of mere display, and called it dealing in borrowed tinsel. But in making that objection he betrayed a protective concern for his own style, which was more elaborate than Hazlitt's, less sudden in its wit or grandeur; a style of amplification rather than sublimity. The distinction between these terms also comes from Longinus, and may help to explain Hazlitt's preferences both as a writer and as an observer of writing. Sublimity occurs as a break or rift in the routine progress of utterance, and the flowing-in of some higher utterance: the work of an instant, and gone in an instant. Amplification works more methodically and with better calculated results. By slow augmentation it may achieve something of comparable power—or rather, something of comparable energy, counted in its total sweep. So, with a grand enough subject, the rhetorical pattern of "The House that Jack Built" might arrive at a power equal to that of the single sentence, "Let there be light." But De Quincey trusted amplification as the only dependable source of eloquence: what he calls (praising himself) "rhythmus, or pomp of cadence, or sonorous ascent of clauses," he suspects is denied to Hazlitt, whose style he calls "(to borrow an impressive word from Coleridge) non-sequacious." Putting the same observation in a light more favorable to Hazlitt, one might say his are the shorter, higher flights, though De Quincey stays longer on the wing. The effect of sublimity, "not persuasion but transport," as Longinus describes it, can hardly be sustained in a manner suitable to a Verrine Oration, or an oriental narrative like De Quincey's "Revolt of the Tartars."

Yet it was shrewd of De Quincey to link Hazlitt's extensive use of quotation with the bursts of eloquence that can seem the distinctive feature of his style. I have mentioned in Hazlitt's defense the Longinian belief that eloquence is the work of memory, a contest with the "souls" of earlier writers who impose themselves on the memory of their successor. But the contrast with De Quincey brings out Hazlitt's agreement with Longinus in a more general assumption: that power is measured by its striving to overcome resistance. Longinus could make oratory the pattern of all eloquence because his ideal community of speech was a republic, in which the speaker's power is freely given, the listener's assent may be withheld, and a rival example of eloquence may arise from any member of the community. He refused for the same reason to suppose that tyranny or oligarchy could ever foster great writing. Sublimity is known by its conversion of the audience, and for the conversion to be real the audience cannot have been bought, or chained to their seats. They must be an audience of equals. Longinus says much of this and implies the rest, in a commonly overlooked passage near the end of *On the Sublime*. Hazlitt confirms it when he writes, "The mind strikes out truth by collision." The phrase gains special force from its context, in his essay "On the Aristocracy of Letters."

> Learning is a kind of external appendage or transferable property—
>
> " 'T was mine, 'tis his, and may be any man's"—
>
> Genius and understanding are a man's self, an integrant part of his personal identity; and the title to these last, as it is the most difficult to be ascertained, is also the most grudgingly acknowledged. . . . Pedants, I will add here, talk to the vulgar as pedagogues talk to school-boys, on an understood principle of condescension and superiority, and therefore make little progress in the knowledge of men or things. . . . There can be no true superiority but what arises out of the presupposed ground of equality: there can be no improvement but from the free communication and comparing of ideas. Kings and nobles, for this reason, receive little benefit from society—where all is submission on one side, and condescension on the other. The mind strikes out truth by collision, as steel strikes fire from the flint!

This was Hazlitt's favorite metaphor of resistance, and he sometimes gave it a bolder emphasis by the cheerless thing he made of its opposite. In *The Spirit of the Age*, after paying his respects to the elegance, learning, and public spirit of Mackintosh's writings, he comes to the single defect which none of these qualities can lighten: "he strikes when the iron is cold." Again, in defending the remark that the French are a nation "void and bare of the faculty of imagination," he dwells on the irreconcilability of continuous finish with unexpected grandeur. Finish affords perfection of a kind; but where no roughness exists, the habitual response will soon find a home; in a nation that cares for Racine more than Shakespeare, there is a soft sediment of presumed understanding, into which even the language of common use pretty comfortably settles.

> The words *charming, delicious, indescribable,* &c. excite the same lively emotions in their minds as the most vivid representations

of what is said to be so; and hence verbiage and the cant of sentiment fill the place, and stop the road to genius—a vague, flaccid, enervated rhetoric being too often substituted for the pith and marrow of truth and nature. The greatest facility to feel or to comprehend will not produce the most intense passion, or the most electrical expression of it. There must be a resistance in the matter to do this—a collision, an obstacle to overcome. The torrent rushes with fury from being impeded in its course: the lightning splits the gnarled oak.

In figures like these Hazlitt represented the energy of mind that he honored in others and sought in himself.

Quotation belongs among the signs of such energy—not only because a writer discloses his own identity partly by declaring his affinities, and quotation is a way of doing so—but also from its resourcefulness as a weapon. Suppose I am embroiled in a controversy with X, the author of a celebrated but unreadable Lay Sermon; we both claim legitimate descent from a great Protestant poet, and know it will add to the respect others feel for us, to be considered his rightful heir. Now, if I can quote him, in his own voice, or what I convince you to be his true voice, more effectively than X, I will have won two battles at once: at the "tribunal of the soul," I am found adequate; and in the rhetorical contest with my rival contemporaries, I have prevailed for the moment. Any interpretation, of course—like Hazlitt's polemical reading of *The Tempest*—can effect a similar double conquest, but for different reasons. There the debate is manifest. (Why do they fight so about Caliban?—Because Caliban had long been a code-name for the lower classes.—But Coleridge only called him "Jacobin"; why then defend him from *that* charge, if the good of the lower classes is what you have at heart?—It looks as if Coleridge were really trying to attach his new anti-Jacobin allegory to the old fear of those classes, and get the combined force of two prejudices by employing a code-word; but it takes a reply like Hazlitt's to make us see this.) Yet with quotation the terms of the debate may themselves be suppressed. The advantage of quoting is simply the advantage of speed and wit—of a particularly compressed sort of interpretation which requires all the reader's ingenuity to unpack.

If one allows quotation the broad sense in which alone it matters to Hazlitt, it comes to seem closely related to echo and allusion. It is one means of advancing the writer's argument while evoking other strengths as the likeness of his own. And it gives the welcome to tradition without which any claim of originality is null. Hazlitt's ease in quoting for the sake of illustration has appeared plainly enough [previously]. The few examples that follow, of quotations not identified, but reshaped as allusions for the sake of argument, fall outside the range of what is normally called literary criticism. They suit my purpose the better for that. After all, one can feel the same doubts in reading a great many other eighteenth- and nineteenth-century critics, and everything Longinus says about the connection between memory and genius, quotation and invention, echo and original, has the aim of warning us that the line had better not be drawn anywhere.

Hannah More remarked of Burke: "How closely that fellow reasons in metaphor!" Modern readers, if they find this a surprising thought, still know what kind of excellence it refers to—the intellectual rigor that impresses us, for example, in a sentence by Johnson on the beginning of Savage's life: "Born with a legal claim to honor and to affluence, he was in two months illegitimated by the parliament, and disowned by his mother, doomed to poverty and obscurity, and launched upon the ocean of life, only that he might be swallowed by its quicksands or dashed upon its rocks"; or in a sentence by Henry James, on a mother's shameless apology to the daughter she has neglected and now wishes to desert in good conscience: "She turned this way and that in the predicament she had sought and from which she could neither retreat with grace nor emerge with credit: she draped herself in the tatters of her impudence, postured to her utmost before the last little triangle of cracked glass to which so many fractures had reduced the polished plate of filial superstition." *Close reasoning* here means the joining of discrete elements in a metaphor that houses them all: by elaboration (the quicksands—the rocks; the glass—the fractures), but also by the improvised movement that justifies the introduction of a metaphor in the first place ("doomed" by a strictly verbal parallel brings forth "launched"; "turned this way and that" makes room for "postured" and so for the imaginary mirror). All this we see, with a little conscious effort, and with pangs unknown to the nineteenth-century reader. What it means to have earned a different compliment—"How closely that fellow reasons in allusion"—may have passed beyond our grasp. But unless we try to make sense of Hazlitt's reasoning-in-allusion, we separate him from a virtue that he ranked very high, and possessed in a high degree: what he liked to call, quoting Dryden, the "o'erinforming power" of style.

I start with an illustration of reasoning loosely taken not from Hazlitt but from a biography of him. It should be plain at the outset that there is nothing intrinsically fine about an allusion; used as a make-weight in any rhetorical balance of fear, to lighten the pretensions of the reader by loading him down with a sense of the author's learning, it is a harmless sort of bullying: among the academic vices, it offers a more limited assault than shouting from the lectern, with a more visible termination than footnotes in Sanskrit. The biographer in this instance, Herschel Baker, has been discussing the effect of Burke's writings on the debate over the French Revolution, an effect Hazlitt described as "tremendous, fatal, such as no exertion of wit or knowledge or genius can ever counteract or atone for." Yet Baker himself has a good deal of sympathy for Burke, and this is important to my sense of the allusion's misfiring; for he writes of Burke: "His sentence was for open war." A careless reader can be expected to go past it quickly, thinking it perhaps an allusion. But the careful reader, who pauses long enough to recall the precise context of the allusion, will pause long enough also to construe its translation into the new setting and to ask what is gained. The original speaker of the line is Moloch, in Book II of *Paradise Lost*, and he says it in the course of another debate about war and revolution. The fallen angels in Pandaemonium are wondering how to deport themselves now that Heaven is lost: Belial wants them to plead for God's mercy; Mammon, to make Hell inhabitable; but Moloch urges a renewal of war against Heaven—"My sentence is for open war."

What has all this to do with Burke? How seriously does Baker intend the comparison between Burke and Moloch, and how seriously can we take it? A scholar of anti-Jacobin sympathies, he probably did not mean to imply a likeness between Burke and the least repentant of the crew assembled in Hell; on the contrary, with more care for the parallels, he would doubtless have preferred to compare the revolutionary metaphysicians of France with Satan, Moloch, and the rest: if we regard Burke as a hero of legitimacy, and really want to translate him into the scheme of *Paradise Lost*, we shall align him with Abdiel. The wrong comparison occurred, however, because this critic *as he wrote* was not aware just what his source did with the words, "His sentence was for open war"; or if he knew, he chose not to think about it. This sort of occurrence, multiplied many times, gives us the "quotey" atmosphere that is so familiar a feature of modern criticism.

An example like this can remind us by negative instruction what happens in a genuine allusion. It will be worked out closely enough for the chosen text to resonate fully both in its original and in its adopted context. Always, the allusion thinks about what it is up to, and lets us see it thinking. Whether the author is conscious of his source may be a less important question than it seems: in either case the act of appropriation brings a new gravity to the new context. The tact is there, and the impression of choice. One is not looking at a chance ornament that the author lunged for with one hand while keeping his fingers crossed in the other. Allusion may therefore be our best evidence of a quality for which we have as yet no good name—a poor one which will serve for the moment is *rhetorical density*—in the command of which Hazlitt's only rivals in prose are Burke and Ruskin. So one can turn De Quincey's comment around, and see it as a resentful version of the praise Hazlitt awarded to Milton: "The quantity of art in him shews the strength of his genius." How richly Hazlitt himself merits this praise will emerge form any careful survey of his practice.

My first example comes from a long footnote midway through the essay "On Paradox and Common-place," on the propensity in all theoretical philosophers, all extreme partisans of a single theory, to react extravagantly against the errors into which their own extravagance has plunged them. The note follows this sentence: "Jacobins or Anti-Jacobins—outrageous advocates for anarchy and licentiousness, or flaming apostles of political persecution—always violent and vulgar in their opinions, they oscillate, with a giddy and sickening motion, from one absurdity to another, and expiate the follies of youth by the heartless vices of advancing age." So far, Hazlitt gives no quotation marks; yet we are aware already of Milton's fallen angels arguing to "no end, in wand'ring mazes lost," and, in much closer reach, Pope's vision of the Hags' Sabbath in the "Epistle to a Lady":

> At last, to follies Youth could scare defend,
> 'Tis half their Age's prudence to pretend;
> Ashamed to own they gave delight before,
> Reduc'd to feign it, when they give no more.

The sentence is quite casual—a passing move, nothing more—and its allusions seem contained in the compositional texture, without ambition for a life of their own. The comparisons with Milton and Pope are far from pointed; they are thought, and felt; not false, but not trying to be significantly true. In the footnote however, there is a sustained allusion, capped by a quotation, which convinces us without mere muscular display that this was the writer's only means of working his will.

> To give the modern reader *un petit aperçu* of the tone of literary conversation about five or six and twenty years ago, I remember being present in a large party composed of men, women, and children, in which two persons of remarkable candour and ingenuity were labouring (as hard as if they had been paid for it) to prove that all prayer was a mode of dictating to the Almighty, and an arrogant assumption of superiority. A gentleman present said, with great simplicity and *naïveté*, that there was one prayer

which did not strike him as coming under this description, and being asked what that was, made answer, "The samaritan's— 'Lord be merciful to me a sinner!' " This appeal by no means settled the sceptical dogmatism of the two disuptants, and soon after the proposer of the objection went away; on which one of them observed with great marks of satisfaction and triumph— "I am afraid we have shocked that gentleman's prejudices." This did not appear to me at that time quite the thing, and this happened in the year 1794. Twice has the iron entered my soul. Twice have the dastard, vaunting, venal crew gone over it; once as they went forth, conquering and to conquer, with reason by their side, glittering like a faulchion, trampling on prejudices and marching fearlessly on in the work of regeneration; once again, when they returned with retrograde steps, like Cacus's oxen dragged backward by the heels, to the den of Legitimacy, "rout on rout, confusion worse confounded," with places and pensions and the Quarterly Review dangling from their pockets, and shouting "Deliverance for mankind," for "the worst, the second fall of man." Yet I have endured all this marching and countermarching of poets, philosophers, and politicians over my head as well as I could, like "the camomoil that thrives, the more 'tis trod upon." By Heavens, I think, I'll endure it no longer!

Here, in small, is the adventure of a generation of poets, philosophers, perfectibilitarians of every sort, Socratic and Pantisocratic, as they sally out to do battle with the enemy and return in defeat (which having changed sides they call victory), while Hazlitt stands watching at the center of the turbulence, somewhere between dissent and subordination, between paradox and commonplace. There are in fact several interlinked allusions; but the drama of this passage owes everything to an image which is made distinct in the quotation, "rout on rout, confusion worse confounded": a fragment of what old Chaos says to Satan about the War in Heaven.

> I know thee, stranger, who thou art,
>   That mighty leading Angel, who of late
>   Made head against Heav'n's King, though overthrown.
> I saw and heard, for such a numerous Host
> Fled not in silence through the frighted deep
>   With ruin upon ruin, rout on rout,
>   Confusion worse confounded.

The quotation gives us a picture of Hazlitt, neither so ancient nor so durable as Night, unable to tolerate the war-whoops and lesser noisemaking of the marchers and counter-marchers, who since they *back into* Hell can think it Heaven. But the grotesque power of his mockery—"places and pensions and the Quarterly Review dangling from their pockets"—suggests also an oblique homage to Pope, whose full-scale allusion to Milton appeared in *The Dunciad*. In this way Hazlitt gathers strength as he goes, by recognizing allies in the middle distance as well those he meant to salute from afar; or rather, his memory seems to do the work for him, as if, coming late in history, it had a certain itinerary to complete.

Some readers may now be ready to protest. It does seem a very full tableau for a single quotation to sketch; if a footnote takes so much art, how can imaginative prose, especially a headlong energetic prose like Hazlitt's, ever get off the ground; for this (the protest concludes) is the undersong of writing, which only criticism troubles about. The objection sounds plausible. Yet apply it to a poetic allusion, which we recognize also as a critical act, and it loses its plausibility. The double standard says a great deal about our distance from Hazlitt. He wrote with an ease of reference we are now so far from taking for granted that when we see it in an older writer of prose, our daily practice gets in the way of our understanding. The impulse that makes us say, or want to say, "He couldn't have worked in all that," belongs to the same family of reflexes at whose bidding we write "the poet T. S. Eliot," to be certain of every reader's confidence. At the very least we want to identify all our quotations. But Hazlitt knew his audience better than that, and had no need to apologize for a strategy of allusion that prose and poetry can share. To quote or allude is, in certain circumstances, an act of invention. And the same goes for any argument from a received trope which modifies, extends, or subverts the trope itself.

A simple instance of this sort of argument may be taken from Hazlitt's debate with Southey over the reasonableness of timely conversions. Southey wrote in defense of his change of heart: "They [the Dissenters] had turned their faces towards the East in the morning, to worship the rising sun, and in the evening they were looking eastward still, obstinately affirming that still the sun was there. I, on the contrary, altered my position as the world went round." But for Hazlitt this metaphor was adaptable to different ends, and by directing it to them he could seem to observe the natural figurative logic of language itself. "It is not always," he replies, "that a simile runs on all-fours; but this does," and one can imagine him thinking here with a murmur of triumph, The Lord has delivered him into my hands: "The sun, indeed, passes from the East to the West, but it rises in the East again; yet Mr. Southey is still looking in the West—for his pension."

Open battles of so blunt a character will seldom tempt either side into the dramatic subtlety of allusion. But to a mind certain of the advantage it gets in arguing from a received trope, allusion will always seem an attractive way of crowding an argument and making implicit alliances by an act of invention that looks like an act of recovery. We all know this trick from our intimate experience of sarcasm in conversation; as when I say to a friend, "Our foreign policy works!" and he replies, "Yes, like the future." Hazlitt, playing with Southey's revolutionary sundown, was correcting a metaphor to make its interest flow all his way, without quite having to allude. Yet this kind of maneuver shares the spirit of allusion. How much so will appear from a similar effect in two sentences of Hazlitt's *Table-Talk* essay on "On Patronage and Puffing," where he imagines the late-won pride of an unhappy dependent. "You are not hailed ashore; as you had supposed, by these kind friends, as a mutual triumph after all your struggles and their exertions on your behalf. It is a piece of presumption in you to be seen walking on *terra firma*; you are required, at the risk of their friendship, to be always swimming in troubled waters, that they may have the credit of throwing out ropes, and sending out life-boats to you, without ever bringing you ashore." One's first thought in reading this is that the situation it describes hardly answers to any Hazlitt could have experienced in his own life. A second thought is that it does, however, fit the life of Johnson; indeed it feels like a conscious allusion to his letter to Lord Chesterfield, which includes the phrase about a patron as "one who looks with unconcern on a man struggling for life in the water, and, when he has reached ground, encumbers him with help." Boswell's *Life*, which first printed the letter, was among Hazlitt's favorite books, even if it would not have seemed to him in a class with Shakespeare or Wordsworth; not, that is, a book which he could properly introduce to readers without quotation marks. But though Boswell may have made a still deeper impression on him than he knew, I prefer to think of his passage as an improvised cadenza on the same metaphor, by a mind in love with metaphorical thinking, and having the letter as part of its accidental store. At any rate one can say that the Patronized Drowning Man is being employed in a way that agrees with Johnson, and with Johnson's context. The reverberations are full where those of Burke-as-Moloch are empty.

There is no clear way of distinguishing unconscious allusion, or allusion that seems to do its work as part of an author's second nature, from *echo* in the sense of that word defined by John Hollander: "echo . . . represents or substitutes for allusion as allusion does for quotation." In practice the first two often merge into a single effect since a reader can estimate how well an echo conceals its work of substitution only from his judgment of the "keeping" between the text and its new context; and nothing but the poetic intelligence every reader creates from the sum of his reading will decide whether a given allusion ought to be honored with the associations of artful distance that the idea of echo includes. As readers we do not sophisticate our guesswork beyond some such rule as this: we want to interpret a passage as echo when by its sound an unsuspected accompaniment is brought into being, which at last we come to think necessary. So, when Hazlitt criticizes the style of the *Rambler* in the style of the *Lives of the Poets*, we hear a profound echo of the later Johnson's manner, cadence, and sense. And when he ventures an echo of poetry it has the power of his best quotations. Consider the following sentence on Coleridge, part of a longer passage I have already quoted from *The Spirit of the Age*: "He who has seen a mouldering tower by the side of a crystal lake, hid by the mist, but glittering in the wave below, may conceive the dim, gleaming, uncertain intelligence of his eye." This presents a familiar array of Coleridgean effects; there, warns Hazlitt, you see what became of his flashing eyes, his floating hair; in their place now is the eye of the mariner, "dim, gleaming, uncertain," and fixed on whomever he encounters. Yet allusion gives the full measure of Hazlitt's genius under different conditions, where several quoted passages can be heard working in concert, all to a single purpose because they direct us to contexts generically allied with each other.

If, as Walter Benjamin argued, quotation always implies an interruption of context, then this sort of composite allusion proceeds by a more complex and interscored series of tonal effects. A writer, gifted with the sense of perfect pitch, interrupts several melodies in which only an ear like his can detect the same signature; he makes of his own recoveries a style we are tempted to describe as pastiche, except that the result adds a new eloquence to what we have known before; with the result that his listening somehow improves ours, and at the same time compels our admiration for the power implied in any sustained act of attentiveness. In the following passage of an 1817 polemic against Southey, it seems to me that Hazlitt does all this. His interruptions have the effect of claiming not only the words but the character who first spoke them for the new context into which they are suddenly imported. The central device of the passage is the personified idea of Legitimacy ("Fine word, Legitimate," Hazlitt says in another place, quoting). The idea is unmasked as Duessa of *The Faerie Queene*, and yet she dominates the allusion very unexclusively. Among the other voices clearly audible are Hamlet in his first and third soliloquies, Leontes in one of his rages, and Timon, self-exiled from the community of men, hoarding his gold and hates. Modern criticism has of course drawn a good many connections among these characters, but none more inevitable than what Hazlitt tells of, as he writes and quotes, answers and listens. A pedant fully imbued with the De Quincean spirit of cavilling might object that the passage is *nothing but* a tissue of paraphrase and quotation. My point is that by the end, as between Hazlitt and the "sources" he gets for kin by serving them as a satisfactory host, we no longer know which is which, and no longer care to ask.

> [Mr. Southey's] engagement to his first love, the Republic, was only upon liking; his marriage to Legitimacy is, *for better, for worse,* and nothing but death shall part them. Our simple Laureate was sharp upon his hoyden Jacobin mistress, who brought him no dowry, neither place nor pension. . . . He divorced her, in short, for nothing but the spirit and success with which she resisted the fraud and force to which the old bawd Legitimacy was forever resorting to overpower her resolution and fidelity. He said she was a virago, a cunning gipsey, always in broils about her honour and the inviolability of her person, and always getting the better in them, furiously scratching the face or cruelly tearing off the hair of the said pimping old lady, who would never let her alone, night or day. But since her foot slipped one day on the ice, and the detestable old hag tripped up her heels, and gave her up to the kind keeping of the Allied Sovereigns, Mr. Southey has devoted himself to her more fortunate and wealthy rival: he is become uxorious in his second matrimonial connexion; and though his false Duessa has turned out a very witch, a foul, ugly witch, drunk with insolence, mad with power, a griping, rapacious wrtech, bloody, luxurious, wanton, malicious, not sparing steel, or poison, or gold, to gain her ends—bringing famine, pestilence, and death in her train—infecting the air with her thoughts, killing the beholders with her looks, claiming mankind as her property, and using them as her slaves—driving every thing before her, and playing the devil wherever she comes, Mr. Southey sticks to her in spite of every thing, and for very shame lays his head in her lap, paddles with the palms of both her hands, inhales her hateful breath, leers in her eyes, and whispers in her ears, calls her little fondling names, Religion, Morality, and Social Order, takes for his motto,
>
> > "Be to her faults a little blind,
> > Be to her virtues very kind"—

sticks close to his filthy bargain, and will not give her up, because she keeps him, and he is down in her will. Faugh!

> "What's here?
> Gold! yellow, glittering, precious gold!
> ———The wappened window,
> Whom the spittle house and ulcerous sores
> Would leave the gorge at, this embalms and spices
> To the April day again."

The above passage is, we fear, written in the style of Aretin, which Mr. Southey condemns in the *Quarterly*. It is at least a very sincere style. . . . Why should not one make a sentence of a page long, out of the feelings of one's whole life.

"That sentence," remarked Keats, "about making a Page of the feelings of a whole life appears to me like a Whale's back in the Sea of Prose." It is true Southey's line on sedition, which required that the rights of certain Englishmen be held in suspense, would have shut down the publications that kept Hazlitt a little ahead of his debts. He was fighting for life. Yet sentences like his are made out of a lifetime of reading; and who that has listened can say where reading ends and feeling begins?

Chronology

1778	William Hazlitt born April 10 at Maidstone, Kent.
1779	The Hazlitts move to Bandon, County Cork, in Ireland.
1783	The Hazlitts sail for America.
1787	Family returns to England, taking up residence at Wem, Shropshire.
1793	William Hazlitt matriculates at Unitarian New College at Hackney, London.
1795	Deciding not to join the ministry, Hazlitt leaves school and returns home.
1798	In January, Hazlitt makes the acquaintance of Samuel Taylor Coleridge. Visits Coleridge and Wordsworth that spring, reading the yet unpublished *Lyrical Ballads*.
1799	Inspired by an exhibition of Italian artists in London, Hazlitt takes up painting.
1802	Hazlitt spends most of his time in Paris, often at the Louvre.
1804	Becomes acquainted with Charles Lamb.
1805	Hazlitt publishes his first book, *Essay on the Principles of Human Action*.
1807	*The Eloquence of the British Senate* is published.
1808	Hazlitt marries Sarah Stoddart.
1809	A son, William, Jr., is born.
1812	Hazlitt gives lectures on English Philosophy. Becomes a journalist with the *Morning Chronicle*.

1814   Publishes with the *Examiner* and *Edinburgh Review*.

1815–17   Becomes politically active as journalist.

1816   Publishes *Memoirs of the Late Thomas Holcroft*.

1817–18   Publishes *The Round Table*; *Characters of Shakespear's Plays*; *Lectures on the English Poets*; *A View of the English Stage*.

1818–19   Gives lectures on English poetry, comic writers, and Elizabethan dramatists.

1819   *Political Essays*; *A Letter to William Gifford*; *Lectures on the English Comic Writers* published.

1820   Writes "Table Talk" for *London Magazine*. *Lectures Chiefly on the Dramatic Literature of the Age of Elizabeth* published.

1821–22   Hazlitt becomes enamored of Sarah Walker.

1822   Hazlitt granted divorce at Edinburgh.

1823   *Characteristics* (aphorisms) and *Liber Amoris* published.

1824   Hazlitt marries the widow Isabella Bridgwater.

1826–27   Publishes *Notes of a Journey Through France and Italy* and *The Plain Speaker*. Separation from second wife.

1828–30   *The Life of Napoleon*.

1830   *Conversations of James Northcote*. On September 18, Hazlitt dies at home, 6 Frith Street, Soho, London.

Contributors

HAROLD BLOOM, Sterling Professor of the Humanities at Yale University, is the author of *The Anxiety of Influence*, *Poetry and Repression*, and many other volumes of literary criticism. His forthcoming study, *Freud: Transference and Authority*, attempts a full-scale reading of all of Freud's major writings. A MacArthur Prize Fellow, he is general editor of five series of literary criticism published by Chelsea House.

STUART M. TAVE, William Rainey Harper Professor of English at the University of Chicago, wrote *The Amiable Humorist* and *Some Words of Jane Austen*.

CHRISTOPHER SALVESEN is the author of *The Landscape of Memory: A Study of Wordsworth's Poetry* and a collection of poems, *Floodsheaf: From a Parish History*.

ROBERT READY teaches English at Drew University. He is the author of *Hazlitt at Table*.

JOHN KINNAIRD is the author of *William Hazlitt: Critic of Power*.

MICHAEL FOOT is the author of *British Foreign Policy Since 1898*, *Men in Uniform*, *Six Faces of Courage*, and (with J. L. Hammond) *Gladstone and Liberalism*.

JOHN L. MAHONEY, Professor of English at Boston College, is the author of *The Logic of Passion: The Literary Criticism of William Hazlitt*.

DAVID BROMWICH, Professor of English at Princeton University, is the author of *Hazlitt: The Mind of a Critic*.

Bibliography

Albrecht, William P. *Hazlitt and the Creative Imagination*. Lawrence: University of Kansas Press, 1965.

————. "Structure in Two of Hazlitt's Essays." *Studies in Romanticism* 21 (Summer 1982): 181–90.

————. *William Hazlitt and the Malthusian Controversy*. Albuquerque: University of New Mexico Press, 1950.

Baker, Herschel Clay. *William Hazlitt*. Cambridge, Mass.: Harvard University Press, 1962.

Bate, Walter Jackson. "William Hazlitt." In *Criticism: The Major Texts*. New York: Harcourt, Brace, 1952.

Brett, R. L. *Hazlitt*, edited by Ian Scott-Kilvert. London: Published for the British Council by Longman Group, 1977.

Bromwich, David. *Hazlitt: The Mind of a Critic*. New York and Oxford: Oxford University Press, 1983.

Bullitt, John M. "Hazlitt and the Romantic Conception of the Imagination." *Philological Quarterly* 24 (October 1945): 343–61.

Carnall, Geoffrey. "The Impertinent Barber of Baghdad: Coleridge's Comic Figure in Hazlitt's Essays." In *New Approaches to Coleridge: Biographical and Critical Essays*, edited by Donald Sultana. Totowa, N.J.: Barnes and Noble, 1981.

Eagleton, Terry. "William Hazlitt: An Empiricist Radical." *Blackfriars* 54 (1973): 108–17.

Eberle, Suzanne Pilat. *William Hazlitt's Art Criticism: An Analogue of French Realism and Impressionism*. Ph.D. diss., University of Detroit, 1980.

Haefner, J. "The Soul Speaking in the Face: Hazlitt's Concept of Character." *Studies in English Literature, 1500–1900* 24 (Autumn 1984): 655–70.

Hassler, Donald J. "The Discovery of the Future and Indeterminacy in William Hazlitt." *The Wordsworth Circle* 8 (Winter 1977): 75–79.

Houck, James A. "Byron and William Hazlitt." In *Lord Byron and His*

Contemporaries: *Essays for the Sixth International Byron Seminar*, edited by Charles E. Robinson. Newark: University of Delaware Press, 1982.

———. *William Hazlitt*: *A Reference Guide*. Boston: G. K. Hall, 1977.

Kinnaird, John William. *William Hazlitt*: *Critic of Power*. New York: Columbia University Press, 1978.

Levin, R. "Hazlitt on Henry V and the Appropriation of Shakespeare." *Shakespeare Quarterly* 35 (Summer 1984): 134–41.

Maclean, Catherine MacDonald. *Born Under Saturn*: *A Biography of William Hazlitt*. London: Collins, 1943.

Mahoney, John L. *The Logic of Passion*: *The Literary Criticism of William Hazlitt*. Rev. ed. New York: Fordham University Press, 1981.

Miller, Edmund G. "Hazlitt and Fawcett." *The Wordsworth Circle* 8 (Autumn 1977): 77–82.

Miller, Stephen. "The Gentleman in the Parlour." *American Scholar* 49 (1979–80): 115–26.

Nabholtz, John R. "Modes of Discourse in Hazlitt's Prose." *The Wordsworth Circle* 10, no. 1 (Winter 1979): 97–106.

O'Hara, J. D. "Hazlitt and Romantic Criticism of the Fine Arts." *Journal of Aesthetics and Art Criticism* 37 (Autumn 1968): 72–85.

Park, Roy. *Hazlitt and the Spirit of the Age*: *Abstraction and Critical Theory*. Oxford: Oxford University Press, 1971.

Patterson, Charles I. "Hazlitt's Criticism in Retrospect." *Studies in English Literature*, *1500–1900* 21 (Autumn 1981): 647–63.

Pearson, Hesketh. *The Fool of Love*: *A Life of William Hazlitt*. London: H. Hamilton, 1934.

Praz, Mario. "Is Hazlitt a Great Essayist?" *English Studies* 13 (1931): 1–6.

Priestly, John Boynton. *William Hazlitt*. Published for the British Council by Longmans, Green and Co., 1960.

Ready, Robert. "Flat Realities: Hazlitt on Biography." *Prose Studies* 5 (December 1983): 309–17.

Ready, Robert. *Hazlitt at Table*. Rutherford: Fairleigh Dickinson University Press, 1981.

———. "Hazlitt: In and Out of 'Gusto.' " *Studies in English Literature*, *1500–1900* 14 (Autumn 1974): 537–46.

Schneider, Elisabeth. *The Aesthetics of William Hazlitt*: *A Study of the Philosophical Basis of His Criticism*. Philadelphia: University of Pennsylvania Press, 1933.

Sikes, Herschel, M. *William Hazlitt's Theory of Literary Criticism in Its Contemporary Application*. Ph.D. diss., New York University, 1957.

Stapleton, Laurence. "William Hazlitt: The Essayist and the Moods of the

Mind." In *The Elected Circle: Studies in the Art of Prose*. Princeton: Princeton University Press, 1973.

Story, Patrick. "Emblems of Infinity: Contemporary Portraits in Hazlitt's *The Spirit of the Age*." *The Wordsworth Circle* 10 (Winter 1979): 81–90.

Verdi, Richard. "Hazlitt and Poussin." *Keats–Shelley Memorial Bulletin* 32 (1981): 1–18.

Voisine, Jacques. "William Hazlitt's Contribution to Romantic Criticism." In *Le Romantisme anglo-américain: mélanges offert à Louis Bonnerot*. Paris: Didier, 1971.

Wardle, Ralph M. *Hazlitt*. Lincoln: University of Nebraska, 1971.

Wellek, René. *Immanuel Kant in England, 1793–1838*. Princeton: Princeton University Press, 1931.

Wells, S. "Shakespeare in Hazlitt's Theatre Criticism." *Shakespeare Survey* 35 (1982): 43–55.

Wright, William C. "Hazlitt, Ruskin, and Nineteenth-Century Art Criticism." *Journal of Aesthetics and Art Criticism* 32 (Summer 1974): 509–23.

Acknowledgments

"Antipathetic and Sympathetic" by Stuart M. Tave from *The Amiable Humorist* by Stuart M. Tave, © 1960 by the University of Chicago. Reprinted by permission of The University of Chicago Press and the author.

"A Master of Regret" (originally entitled "Introduction") by Christopher Salvesen from *Selected Writings of William Hazlitt* by Christopher Salvesen, © 1972 by Christopher Salvesen. Reprinted by permission of Signet/New American Library.

"The Logic of Passion: *Liber Amoris*" (originally entitled "The Logic of Passion: Hazlitt's *Liber Amoris*") by Robert Ready from *Studies in Romanticism* 14 (Winter 1975), © 1975 by the Trustees of Boston University. Reprinted by permission.

"The Modern Difference: Comedy and the Novel" by John Kinnaird from *William Hazlitt: Critic of Power* by John Kinnaird, © 1978 by Columbia University Press. Reprinted by permission of the publisher.

"The Shakespeare Prose Writer" by Michael Foot from *Debts of Honour* by Michael Foot, © 1980 by Michael Foot. Reprinted by permission.

"Imagination and the Ways of Genius" by John L. Mahoney from *The Logic of Passion: The Literary Criticism of William Hazlitt* by John L. Mahoney, © 1978 by John L. Mahoney. Reprinted by permission of Fordham University Press.

"The Egotistical Sublime: Wordsworth and Rousseau" (originally entitled "The Egotistical Sublime") by David Bromwich from *Hazlitt: The Mind of a Critic* by David Bromwich, © 1983 by Oxford University Press. Reprinted by permission.

"The Politics of Allusion" by David Bromwich from *Hazlitt: The Mind of a Critic* by David Bromwich, © 1983 by Oxford University Press. Reprinted by permission.

Index